SLACKWATER

P J BOOTH

SLACKWATER
Published in 2020 by Peter John Booth
Copyright © Peter John Booth 2020
ISBN 978-164826136-7

The right of Peter John Booth to be identified as the author of this work has been asserted in accordance with the Copyright Act 1968 (Australia). No part of this publication may be reproduced, stored in a retrieval system, or transmitted in any form or by any means, electronic, mechanical, photocopying, recording or otherwise, without the prior written permission of the author.

Dedication

For Helen, Amelia-Rose and Nicholas

Slackwater

Chapter 1	The Fisherman	7
Chapter 2	The Molly	15
Chapter 3	The rhythm of the Bay	21
Chapter 4	Selling the catch, now and then	25
Chapter 5	The old days	27
Chapter 6	Boat maintenance, the Bantam and the Handbag	31
Chapter 7	Port Melbourne	35
Chapter 8	The House	37
Chapter 9	The milk bar	41
Chapter 10	Risky business	45
Chapter 11	A morning fishing	47
Chapter 12	The Pub	51
Chapter 13	The regulars	55
Chapter 14	Oleg the Russian	59
Chapter 15	The bar	61
Chapter 16	The food in the pub	65
Chapter 17	Body or bag	69
Chapter 18	A visit to the Warthog	75
Chapter 19	Craypots, octopus and eels	81
Chapter 20	The Fisherman is thrown from the boat	85
Chapter 21	Local politics	89
Chapter 22	The hardware shop	95
Chapter 23	Back at the pub	99
Chapter 24	Mending the nets and a visit from Spud	103
Chapter 25	A trip up the river and the last eel fisher	107
Chapter 26	The fish restaurant	113
Chapter 27	The fisheries inspector	115
Chapter 28	Greek Easter	119
Chapter 29	A job for Skinny	123
Chapter 30	The stingray in the net	131
Chapter 31	Painless	135
Chapter 32	The incident in the lane	143
Chapter 33	The next day	149
Chapter 34	Murray comes to the house	155
Chapter 35	The frozen Russian and the run down the Bay	161
Chapter 36	Slackwater	165
Chapter 37	The run home	169
Chapter 38	Oleg says goodbye	175
Chapter 39	The singer in the bar	177
Chapter 40	The Russians pay a visit	179

Slackwater

Chapter 1

The Fisherman

He snapped the fish's neck quickly and efficiently, as he had done so many times before. He quickly cut its throat and bled it over the side so the flesh would not become tainted. With a backhand flip of the wrist, the fish spun into the old wooden box in the hold of the boat.

"Fuck..." he said quietly to himself... "salmon."

He brought the net over the transom with a slow steady motion, pausing briefly to remove a fish now and then. Each fish was dispatched with an economy of movement. Occasionally the silence was broken by the phrase "Fucking salmon" or just "Fuck".

The net coiled on itself in the bottom of the boat, shiny with water.

A large gummy shark came struggling over the transom, tail thrashing in a froth of water. He pinned it to the deck with his fist and wrestled it from the net. A sharp blow to the head with the old ebony ruler and it was subdued. Quickly bled over the side of the boat, it was tossed into the box.

His mood slightly improved, at least the shark was worth some money, unlike the salmon which he virtually gave away, such was the lack of demand.

His watch, salty and scratched with its faded web strap, told him it was still early. Time to set the net again he thought.

The old Yanmar diesel clattered into life and he motored slowly to another spot where he usually had some luck. The early morning was still dark so he could not navigate by his normal marks, land-based features which he triangulated by eye. The small depth sounder under the stern deck told him which way to go. There were some advantages to technology, despite his attempts to remain indifferent to it in all its manifestations, especially depth sounders and navigation aids. He refused to use a GPS to navigate. He knew where he was going and used the marks on the horizon all around him as his guides. He needed nothing else. When it was dark, he used the compass and the feel of the boat as it moved through the water. Occasionally he would use his grandfather's old sounding line to check the depth. Handmade from whipcord, waxed with a 10-pound lead weight on the end. It had markers woven into the whipcord every yard, so one could count when the line was hauled in. Every 10 feet the marker was red, so you could count the depth more easily. He did not use it often, only when he lost his bearings, which was not often. He knew the Bay, its shoals and channels like the back of his hand.

It was still dark when he arrived at his mark. He cut the motor and set the net quietly using the momentum of the boat. The last float over the side, he poured some coffee from the old metal vacuum flask. Dented and scratched from years of use. The coffee was barely warm but still good. A cold cooked sausage and a cold boiled potato left over from last night's dinner made for a welcome break.

The mark was over a small reef which he had fished for years. It was quite productive but too small for larger boats to bother with. He said a silent prayer to the Fish God, asking for a snapper or two, perhaps a half dozen whiting. He did not think that was an unreasonable request having regard to the shit catches lately.

Salmon and mullet were reasonably prolific and able to be caught for most of the year. Snapper and whiting were much less so and confined to spring and summer. The top reaches of the Bay did not fish as well as the bottom reaches. However, he seldom made the long run to the bottom of the Bay, as he had done so many times in his youth.

He finished his meal and drank the now cold coffee from the battered steel flask. The sun suddenly broke the horizon in a blaze of orange as he watched silently.

Soon he set to work cleaning and scaling the fish in the box. Guts were flicked over the side to the ravenous gulls, now floating eagerly behind him. "Choke on that you bastards," he said happily.

He sluiced the deck clean with seawater from an old metal bucket tied to an even older rope. The bilge pump coughed and started automatically. It spat out bilge from the stern, oily and pink at the same time. The rainbow slick drifting away slowly, the surface of the water like glass in the early morning.

He washed his hands with the cold seawater, drying them on the front of his trousers, stiff with salt.

Chapter 1

The boat had drifted silently some way from the net as he had intended. Now he coaxed the old diesel into life. With a cough and clatter, and a billow of black smoke, it started. Time for a service he thought to himself, maybe not just yet though. He would take the boat out of the water soon and get Yanni to service the old diesel.

Yanni, the old Greek mechanic, had a small workshop in the next street. He assumed that Yanni was short for some Greek name, Yiannou or similar. Most people called him Yanni or Wrench which he seemed to prefer. Yanni did not charge a lot for a service. However, each time he took the boat to Yanni, there were mutterings about things to be replaced. He did not have the money for a new engine. Yanni knew that and was adept at finding old parts or adapting others to fit. As long as he was putting about in the top of the Bay, he was content to have the motor running on one cylinder rather than two. If need be, he would put up the sail and drift home as his father and grandfather had done. The motor was added by his father in the late 1950s when sailing became too slow for modern times.

He cut the motor and drifted over to the net. The old boat hook slid under the fish float and he began to haul in the net. A steady hand over hand pull, while coiling it in the bottom of the boat, brought it in quietly.

By now the sun was well over the horizon and the water glinted and sparkled as it fell from the net. The promise of a new day and a full net were as shiny as the water. His mood lifted as it always did when he was bringing in the net. Even after all the years, some optimism if not enjoyment at the simple pleasures of fishing remained.

A small snapper broke the surface, entangled in the net. Flapping and splashing, he carefully untangled it. Full of wounded pride and embarrassment the fish was shiny and sleek, its long dorsal fin a row of nasty spikes. The pink hue on its flanks gave it the colloquial name, pinkie.

It was a good sign and he was almost happy. Where small fish were found, usually larger ones were not far away. He knew it was undersized just by looking at it, but he checked anyway. The old plastic measuring ruler secured onto the transom by his grandfather was long gone. These days he used the notches cut into the gunwale by his father. The short one for whiting, the middle one for salmon and mullet and the long one for snapper. Not even legal as a mullet, he tossed it well back away from the gulls so it would have a chance. "Fuck you", he said to the gulls who glared at him with malevolent eyes. "Catch your own", he said. The gulls replied with a chorus of indignant squawks.

Another haul of the net brought in two more undersize pinkies and one just legal. He returned the undersize fish over the side, making sure the gulls were avoided. The legal-sized fish was quickly despatched and flicked into the box. He was becoming almost cheerful although the net was only halfway in.

A good-sized gurnard followed, stocky and spikey but beautiful orange with the classic blue and yellow butterfly pectoral fins. One of the prettiest fish in the sea and one of the best eating. Sadly, the market for gurnard was limited. It was so unusual looking that the housewives from Brighton could not bring themselves to buy one. Hopefully, he would sell it to the local restaurants or maybe the pub. A few more barely legal pinkies and three good size gurnards followed. All went into the box together with a slurry of ice and saltwater.

The remainder of the catch consisted of yellow-eye mullet and a few salmon. All nice sized fish, fat and sleek. He cursed each one as they were tossed into the fish box. "Fucking mullet ...", "Fucking salmon ...", "... Bastard ...". He was even-handed with his derision and equally vehement regardless of either species.

His grandfather had fished these same waters and made a living from barracouta or couta as they were known. An oily fish with beautiful aquamarine marbled flanks, they were caught in great numbers. In his grandfather's day they were the staple of working-class people. Grilled fresh or smoked, they were a wholesome fish which were cheap. Salmon and mullet were also very popular. However, those days were long gone.

The boat he still used had been bought by his grandfather expressly to catch barracouta. Couta boats were seaworthy and fast but could carry good loads of fish in the hold. His father had made a living catching couta as well but by the time he had retired the market for couta had almost gone.

White fleshed fish like snapper and kingfish had become the market leaders. Oily fish like couta, mullet and salmon were very hard to sell.

Chapter 1

After his father retired, the market for oily fish kept declining. But the fishing for snapper was good until the 1970s when the scallop boats began to overfish the Bay. The box dredges ripped up the seabed like a plough destroying the reefs which fed the snapper. The snapper fled the Bay in protest and the fishery all but collapsed. Times were very hard for the Bay fishermen, especially in the top of the Bay.

He took to fishing the bottom of the Bay, making the long run from Port Melbourne each night. For a while he was able to make ends meet but the bottom of the Bay soon became less prolific. He switched to kingfish which, by that time, had become a desirable restaurant fish. The best and most reliable fishing ground for kingfish was the Rip. Not many professionals fished the Rip, it being widely considered to be too dangerous and unpredictable. He was one of the few who fished the Rip routinely and it was good fishing. The fishing was hard and dangerous, but the catches were usually good.

He came to know the Rip and the run down from the Bay from Port Melbourne like the back of his hand, often making the run while half asleep, especially on the way home. However, the Rip was not always reliable and there were times when he used his nautical skills for purposes other than fishing. Syd the Squid would call him from time to time and offer him a job, either 'body' or 'bag'. Each was a term referring to illicit pick-ups from foreign vessels usually in the Rip. A 'body' job was a shivering seaman in the forecastle of the boat. A 'bag' job was a pick-up of a package thrown over the stern of a container boat on a dark night in the Rip. He never looked inside. Both were good money, but he did not like the work at all. After a few years, the scallop dredges were banned in the Bay and the fishing picked up. He preferred fishing to the body or bag trade. It was safer and made him feel less uneasy.

Syd was very disappointed with him when he went back to fishing and still offered him the odd job. Sometimes he said yes; but each time he said it was the last. "You said that last time," Syd would say. "Get fucked," he would reply.

A dolphin surfaced and started nosing around the net. He quite liked dolphins, unlike seals they had a friendly disposition. At least he liked to think so. He had liked dolphins since he was a child. Whenever he saw them, he would feed them with a fish or two. His father did not like them but tolerated his affection for the animals, if only to try and create a bond with the boy. In truth, his father did not like dolphins and, like most fishermen, saw them as a competitor, if not a pest.

As time went on the Fisherman became more affectionate towards the dolphins. He saw them as a token of goodwill and a bringer of fish. If dolphins were about then he knew the fish would follow. The truth was probably quite different. Dolphins were intelligent and knew where to find a free feed. In truth, all the fish were declining so a dolphin had to make do with a Fisherman's net or simple goodwill.

At all events, he tossed the dolphin a mackerel. It was gone in a gulp. The dolphin chittered and was gone with barely a swirl of water. So much for a partnership between man and dolphin.

Some may think the chittering of a dolphin was a thank you. He would have liked to think so. However, he knew that was dolphin for "thanks for the fish, … loser", as they ate your fish and swam away. But he just liked to look at them. If they came to the boat, he fed them so that they would stay, at least for a while. They were company on the long days spent in the boat.

He set a course for home and rigged a few silver blade lures out on long lines. With a little luck he would pick up a kingfish or two. A kingfish would help as they brought quite good money at the markets or restaurants these days.

He turned to the remaining salmon and other fish in the boxes. They were very bloody fish which must be bled and gutted immediately, before the flesh deteriorated. He worked quietly and efficiently, a backhand throw of guts over the side the only punctuation to his work.

The gulls squawked and fought for the guts which twisted in the wake. The only good use for salmon is burley, he thought to himself. Nonetheless, he treated the fish respectfully as he would any animal which he had killed. He slid the fish into a slurry of ice and seawater in order to keep them as fresh as possible.

The diesel clacked noisily in the background, the fumes filling the cockpit.

In the past, a few boxes of salmon or mullet would make a modest profit for the trip. These days it would not break even. Once again, he

Chapter 1

would make a loss on the trip as diesel had become so expensive. He could not recall when he had made a good profit on a trip. Indeed, he could barely remember the good days, they were so long ago.

He was relieved when the motor started, belching black smoke. The sun was well above the horizon and he turned for home. The tiller was set with an old rope tied to the stern at one end. The run home was not long, but it might produce a big fish if he was lucky. He threw a handline with a metal blade lure flashing at the end. You cannot catch a fish if there is no gear in the water, he could hear his father say.

Indeed, his grandfather had said the same thing. Unfortunately, it did not seem to make much difference these days. The lure bounced and flashed in the water just like it was supposed to do. The fish, if they were there, did not do what they were supposed to do. He cleaned and scaled the fish, tossing the guts to the gulls screeching and diving in the wake.

He took each fish from the box and placed it on the board. It was scaled quickly and efficiently. The first cut was from the vent to the throat. The entrails were removed with a second flick of the knife. The next cut was from behind the gill plate and pectoral fins, from neck to throat. One cut. One cut only.

The third cut was along the backbone down to the tail. The last cut was from the neck to the tail, through the rib bones. The final step was to remove the bones and belly. Once again, one cut. A simplicity of motion.

Last of all he would clean and dry his gear. Knives were washed and carefully packed, hooks and lures replaced in old tobacco tins, sinkers in an old coffee tin and lines coiled and fastened to wooden spools. He took special care with the ebony ruler and the gaff.

One of his grandfather's prized possessions was a piece of ebony 18 inches long, a circular leather thong drilled through one end which he would loop around his wrist. It had been given to him by a client who had managed the local bank after the bank had decided that the round ebony rulers used to roll down the pages of the ledgers were old-fashioned and needed to be replaced by flat wooden or aluminium rulers. The old rulers were made of ebony, one of the hardest woods imaginable so that they would never wear out. Banks are like that, they do not like spending money and if they have to, they only like spending it once. The rulers were circular, not flat, so the clerks could roll them down the page, liberating each line in the ledger one at a time in order to be annotated and, occasionally, deleted. His grandfather had, with not inconsiderable effort, drilled a hole in one end of the ebony ruler and tied through a leather thong. Looped around his wrist, it efficiently dispatched even the most unwilling of fish although he reserved it mostly for the larger uncooperative sharks which occasionally disturbed the nets. Almost 90 years later notwithstanding the ravages of salt and sun, the ebony ruler was as hard and unyielding as it ever had been, although the Fisherman had replaced the leather thong several times. That is not to say that it had not always been used to subdue unruly fish. From time to time in his grandfather's day and later his father's day it had been deployed to settle territorial misunderstandings regarding fishing territory and netting rights. These misunderstandings usually took place in the predawn hours, out of sight of land and curiously were never reported to the police.

Similarly, his grandfather's handmade fish gaff had been one of his grandfather's most loved possessions and, then his father's. It was in a pocket under the gunwale hanging from two hooks. His grandfather had made it from a hardwood pole six feet long, a cast-iron shark hook and whip cord. Much of the fishing tackle in his grandfather's day and and even his father's, had been handmade. Nets were woven from wax cotton rope, floats were hand cut from cork, and sinkers were cast from lead sheets taken from old car batteries. The gaff was a vicious thing, the point of the hook honed on a whetstone by his grandfather, so it was razor-sharp and able to penetrate sandpaper skin of a shark with ease. Painted bright red with red enamel paint it had been used for other things on occasion but not by the Fisherman and to his knowledge not since the notorious salmon netting wars of the late 1940s. Nonetheless, it was a comfort to him to have it tucked under the gunwale in case he ever needed it. Just like his father's 303 rifle and the Heckler and Koch pistol in the concealed compartment. You just never know when you might need something like that, he would often say to himself.

Chapter 2

The Molly

The 'Molly' had been bought by his grandfather. Named after his grandmother, Molly, although he did not know until years after she died that her name was not 'Molly' but Winifred. She hated the name as did each of her four sisters. Each had a given name which they abandoned in their early years, taking another which they were known by: Faye, June, Judy, Molly and Peg were how they were known. Few knew their real names. Nonetheless, 'Molly' was a classic couta boat, 26 foot 6 inches in length, a beam of 10 feet and a draft of 3 foot 3 inches. She was gaff rigged with 600 square feet of sail; each sail dyed a diesel rusty brown as was the fashion in those days.

Couta boats were unique to Port Phillip Bay; they were built and designed locally. Fast under sail but seaworthy, they could fish even in rough seas and race back to port. The large amount of deck and deep well in the centre kept the crew dry. They were made of New Zealand Kauri on a hardwood frame. Built by Lacco in Queenscliff in 1914, Molly was a classic mix of working boat and elegant sailboat.

For the last 50 years it had been called XF Z291, commercial boat nomenclature. It was a couta boat and had been built in 1925 by the best couta boat yard in Victoria. They were built to be fast and catch barracouta, the cold-water fish in great numbers outside Port Phillip Heads and to a lesser extent inside Port Phillip Bay. The boats were designed and built in the late 1890s in Queenscliff and were capable of sailing through the Heads and fishing outside in the best "couta" grounds. They were very seaworthy and stable, as were required of boats which had to traverse The Rip, as Port Phillip Heads were known. The boats were of 25 feet in length or thereabouts, although some were about 22 feet in length and some up to 27 feet long. They were about 10 feet wide with a draft of about 3 feet. They had a foredeck, side decks and an aft deck. Such was the design that they kept quite dry even during heavy seas. They were clinker built with a steel centre plate, heavy ballast, often plated with New Zealand Kauri over hardwood keels with a celery top pine deck. Powered by sail, with a gaff rig and two main sails, they would drive hard through the Rip even in rough conditions. Properly trimmed and sailed they were fast and dry. Just the sort of boat needed to quickly get out through the Heads, catch a haul of fish and come back through the Rip, especially if the conditions had deteriorated.

The sail configuration was simple, a single halyard to be used as both a peak and hoist. One person could sail a couta boat. This was very useful so that the other person (there were usually only "two men up") could gut, scale, and split the fish before returning to market. Couta were not fish which improved after being caught. They needed to be gutted and bled quickly before they deteriorated. Not a good thing for market. The cockpit of the boat was deep, set below a deep deck with a rounded coaming to prevent spray and wash from the flooding cockpit. Rowlock blocks were fitted so that the boat could be propelled by oars if need be, as was often the case to set the net if the wind had died. With a light breeze the net could be set and then the boat tacked back to retrieve it, hopefully containing fat couta, salmon or gar.

The gaff rigged mainsail was introduced sometime in the 1900s, making the boats easier to handle and probably faster. A few jibs of different weights made the boat somewhat more amenable to changes in wind speed. Small diesel engines were introduced sometime after the First World War - prior to that the boats were solely powered by sail. However, the diesel engines gave the boats a versatility which they had not had before. They were useful as cray boats or for shark fishing, both of which prospered in the post war period in Port Phillip Bay.

The introduction of the outboard motor and fibreglass construction was the death knell of the working couta boats until their resurgence in the 1960s and 1970s as pleasure boats. Nonetheless, Molly had been built by one of the most prominent builders of couta boats of the day. She had not been purchased by his grandfather as a new boat, but as a used boat. Such was his grandfather's perspicacity. It was bought at a time when the couta haul was good, the market for couta, salmon and gar was at its peak. The boat was renamed "Molly" and fitted with new sails. His father had used the boat until the period after World War II when it was refitted with a small diesel engine. Nothing else had been changed, the mast, sails and rigging were retained. Indeed, they were used often by the Fisherman when conditions were right to save fuel, an important consideration.

Soon thereafter, due to good catches and market prices, the cold or wet well was added under the floor. This was done by raising the floor slightly and adding a hatch. The boat did not sail as well thereafter if it had a full well, but it was worth it for the market prices, the fish being markedly fresher and better looking. When the Fisherman was fishing and the catch was good, he would use the fish well. If the fishing was not so good, and he was close to the mooring, he would use the wooden boxes, built by his grandfather in which to keep the fish. At other times, and for other purposes, now and then he would use the fish well, and another special compartment under the floor which no one else knew about, depending on whether he had a cargo of "body" or "box". But he did not like those runs, at least not when he had a choice.

By the time the boat came to him it was tired but still good. He would spend the winter days, in the weak sun, stripping the boards, re-caulking the joints and antifouling the hull. The latter was not really all that important because he would bring the boat out as soon as he could from the water, and depending on conditions, usually over winter. He did not work fish weekends, not because he was a man of leisure, but because he did not want to engage with the weekend fishing heroes with their 16 foot "plastic fantastics" as he called them, their habits and their general behaviour offended his sense of ownership of the upper Bay. He thought it was better if they had the run of the upper reaches over the weekend. The Bay was his for the rest of the week. It was better that way.

In the beginning, Molly was entirely sail powered, save for when the oars were used to set the net. Although not the fastest couta boat of her time, she could hold her own with most on the way back to port. The first boat into port always sold the catch for the best prices so the competition to enter port first was fierce. Molly would arrive in good time to sell her catch, although rarely the first. His grandfather preferred to stay a while longer and have a larger catch than be first in the market with a smaller haul of fish.

After the Second World War, Molly was fitted with a small diesel motor. The motor was noisy and smoky but a sign of great modernity which his father thought was important. In any event most of the other couta boats had by that time all been fitted with motors, such were the times. Molly was about the last, his grandfather holding on to the old ways as long as he could. His father fished from Molly as his grandfather had done. Little was done to Molly, although in the 1950s, the post-war diesel was replaced with a more modern variety. The motor was close to worn out now, but he kept it going with Yanni's help. It was sufficient for his needs and rarely broke down. The runs to the Rip were seldom made and if needed, he quite enjoyed sailing. The sails and oars were always on the boat just in case they were needed. He took pride in keeping them in good repair as he did with the boat generally.

Molly was the last couta boat commercially fishing the upper Bay and one of only a few left commercially fishing in the Bay. At one time there had been dozens of couta boats in the upper reaches of the Bay. The sight of the fleet running for home with rusty brown sails full of wind was something that few could remember.

He kept Molly on a mooring close in shore at Port Melbourne. The mooring was originally an old engine block which had been sunk by his grandfather. He still used it today although the Council charged him for it. The wooden dinghy his grandfather used as a tender was still seaworthy if only just. He rowed it slowly over the 200 metres to shore.

During winter Molly would be taken ashore and serviced. New antifouling paint on the hull, the deck stripped, re-caulked and oiled. Yanni had a tractor and would back the trailer his grandfather had built over the sand at high tide to drive the boat back to Yanni's yard. Once the motor had been serviced, Yanni would obligingly tow the boat to the Fisherman's home where it would sit in the big shed or on the street, depending on the weather and what needed to be done. He preferred sanding and painting in the open air on account of the fumes.

If the weather was bad, he would get Yanni to put the boat in the shed so he could work on it without getting wet. The boat was never out of the water for long, being needed to earn a livelihood. However, he quite liked the solitary time in the shed, quietly making repairs as needed. A small wood burning stove in the corner providing some warmth on the bitterly cold days.

Sometimes Yanni would take the boat to the beach on a dark night, a body or bag job having been accepted. Those days were mostly gone now, but not entirely. Molly still had some modifications which he and Yanni had made to facilitate such trips. Sails dyed an even darker rust

Chapter 2

brown, almost invisible at night. The hull painted in a dark French navy, almost black. An exhaust bypass on the engine which would, once engaged, render the motor almost silent. A compartment under the floor which would accommodate a body or a bag if need be. He was particularly proud of the joinery. It had taken weeks to get it right, night after night over one winter in the privacy of the shed. It was so perfect that it was invisible, especially at night. His father's 303 rifle was in the compartment, wrapped in oilskins and coated in grease. When he was busy with body or bag jobs, he had added his old Heckler & Koch 9mm semi-automatic pistol. Just in case.

He had used the Heckler & Koch when he was in Vietnam. He had been selected to undertake missions that no one talked about, even then. He had no qualms about killing, although he did not enjoy it. It was a consequence of being a professional fisherman he liked to think. He had taken the Heckler & Koch from a Vietnamese army captain after he had killed him with a double-edged knife, thrust into his heart and rolled his body into the long grass.

Slackwater

Chapter 3

The rhythm of the Bay

Each year from spring until late summer, when the moon was high and the wind was low, snapper would travel up the Bay to spawn.

They arrived in great numbers having amassed outside the Heads in the deep drop offs. They came from Bass Strait where they had roamed and fed, following the deep currents that took them far away from land. Each year they returned to the place where they had been born, the warm, shallow waters of Port Phillip Bay. It was a marvel that they returned to the same water each spawning season but return they did. Unerringly, on time, and in numbers. Following the currents, the temperature or the magnetic field or God knows what. The Fisherman did not care, all it meant to him was good fishing, and plenty of it.

They came as smaller fish, several years old having only gone to sea for the first time. They came as old men of the sea, complete with the massive skull and forehead that only the great old fish have. They came as every other fish in between; such was the compulsion to breed and return to the place where they had spent years as juveniles. The snapper run had waned over decades, no doubt he thought, due to big boats and overfishing. He never took too many, nor had his father or grandfather. They only took what they could sell, even in times when the Bay was so thick with fish you could walk to Williamstown, his father would say. Leave some for next year, he would say gently. He tempered the young man's enthusiasm to catch them all. Sadly, those days were gone and had been for many years. The reducing catch each year had been explained by reference to tides, moons, plastic bags, trawlers and immigrants. Yet each year was worse than which that had been gone.

Now the fishing was poor with a catch of a few fish to be proclaimed as a great day. He knew that it was not a great day and that not even the good days would ever return. His fishing these days had a sadness to it which he felt in his bones but would never speak of. Flathead, on the other hand, were ubiquitous and easy to catch. They ate almost anything, and these days were a table fish of almost evangelical proportions - not bad for a fish that no one wanted for decades. Only the poor people and the Fisherman knew that flathead was one of the best eating fish in the sea. Its monumentally bad looks had kept the fashionable buyers from understanding its great eating qualities.

However, the demand for cheap, clean, white fleshed fish meant that sooner or later the flathead were discovered. This, of course, was good news for the Fisherman. Suddenly the fish which had almost been given away was the main cash catch. But as with all things, it was quickly overfished and soon only the juveniles were left. Day after day he would catch undersized flathead, only to throw them back as he was required to do. A waste of bait, he would mutter and move on, looking for a profitable catch. The trawlers took more than their fair share, even these days. Yet as ever, when one market closed, another seemed to open. Stargazer were fat, lazy bottom dwelling fish, even by flathead standards. They were caught when retrieving the net because they were too lazy to have avoided it. The Fisherman knew that stargazer was a good eating fish but knew that it could never be sold commercially. They were so grotesque that they made flathead look handsome. However, they bore a strong resemblance to monkfish, a northern hemisphere table fish of huge acclamation; despite its looks. Northern hemisphere television chefs promoted monkfish. Smart southern hemisphere fishmongers rebadged stargazer as a monkfish and soon it was outselling flathead as a premium fish. The Fisherman targeted them, or tried to, but they were extremely difficult to catch. They remained elusive to him. When one did tumble into his net, he usually ate it for dinner, the locals refusing to pay what the cognoscenti paid at the South Melbourne markets.

Mackerel were everywhere, so too mullet, salmon and barracouta. The markets for such fish had collapsed years ago with the rise of television chefs and white fleshed fish. Squid, or calamari, as they were now called, had become his staple. It was a long way from the days when they were caught as bait for snapper, now they were revered by migrants and yuppies alike. Best of all, they were plentiful and easy to catch. Whilst they were easier caught and in great numbers at night, they could be caught during the day and often in poor weather. Squid had become his salvation, a matter he would have laughed out loud 10 years before.

He knew the Bay as only a lifetime of fishing could do. He knew that the squid would be on the break between sand and weed, hiding in the weeds and ambushing small fish on the sand flat. He knew where the big snapper would cruise at the 60-foot mark in the channels. Sometimes

Chapter 3

on a full moon they would come into the shallow reefs where he would wait for them. He would net garfish in the still winter mornings near the old wreck. He would bag mussels from the old Fort when times were tough. He knew where the blue mackerel schooled in the deep water off the headlands and that they were best caught in the spring. The young blokes drove their boats fast to a destination, a mark on their depth sounder or GPS, ignoring everything on the way. He fished on the way to a destination, knowing what he would find along the way. He could catch fish, mackerel, flathead and the occasional stargazer while making his way to where he knew the kingfish or snapper would be roaming. Although these days the reality was that the fish were more often "should be" or "were once upon a time".

On lean days, he would longline for Australian salmon or Bay trout as they were called, like he used to in the old times. They were not very profitable but some of the old migrants in Port Melbourne still wanted them. On moonlit nights he would run small nets for mullet either grey or yellow eye, whatever was about.

He made his own squid and fish lures, carved from pine, painted in various colours and with treble hooks screwed on. He used patterns that his father had made in the 1930s. The fish did not know that they were not $35 lures from a chain of tackle shops spruiked by a bloke on a TV program. He filed the hooks with his grandfather's files and finished them with a whetstone. "There is nothing sharper in the sea than my hooks," his father used to say. Whether that was right or not, did not matter, he still made his own lures and sharpened his own hooks. No chemically sharpened Japanese hooks for him at $30 a packet.

On a Sunday morning he would darn and mend his nets, after washing and hanging them on the side fence and on the old clothesline, a Hills hoist for those who could remember them. In the old days he would nurse a beer whilst he did the mending. These days there was tea with plenty of milk and sugar, better yet, condensed milk.

When times were especially lean but not lean enough to do runs to the Rip, he would fish through the night around the wharves at the river mouth. He would catch big bull bream, occasionally jewfish – bright shiny silver slab-sided bastards who ran deep and fought slow and long. They were such beautiful fish he could hardly bring himself to kill them. But he did and they sold well. He would also catch big fat eels in the upper reaches of the rivers, beyond the salt and into the brackish, dark oily water when they grew fat, slimy and mean. But night fishing was for young men, not old men with arthritic knees and bad backs. He would sip tea from the old battered thermos flask and massage his knee. The nagging pain never went away and became particularly bothersome in the cold weather. Night fishing was for young men, every time he went night fishing, he said that to himself. Yet when times were bad, he went back to it. Each time was worse than the last. Each time he swore it was the last. Each time.

One night, the reel screamed and the line raced off the spool at a great rate. It was not a jewfish, or an eel, and bream did not come that big. He said to himself it must be a snapper, but it was bigger than he had caught in many a year, if indeed it was. It went straight for the pylons where it knew the mussels were thick and sharp on the pillars holding up the wharf. He put as much drag on the line as he could, all the while praying the line did not break. He managed to turn its head and it started to parallel zigzag, all the while shaking his head. It was a snapper all right, and a good one. He brought it in and finally, after what seemed a lifetime, up to the surface. When he finally shone a light on it, he drew his breath. It was at least 15 kg and with the beautiful shiny silver and red head of a mature fish. He netted it with one hand while balancing the rod with the other. As soon as he had it in the boat his heart sank. It was a female and clearly gravid, full of eggs. The season rules prevented taking such a fish. He hesitated long and hard, looking at the fish. It would be so easy, restaurants would not care even if they could tell the difference between a bull snapper and a doe. Sadly, he released the fish, quick as always, but this time tinged with regret. Afterwards he felt better knowing that the fish was spawning and helping his fishery prosper. However, it did not overtake his financial regret which was very real.

Chapter 4

Selling the catch, now and then

When he was a boy, he well remembered the fish market on the pier. All the local fishermen would unload their catches onto the pier. The catch was sold by weight as a mixed bag of fish. Sometimes if the catch had been good it was sold by species – bream, salmon, couta, and snook. Sometimes it would be jewfish and whiting, the latter being the most prized of all fish after snapper. Later, this local life disappeared as the Melbourne markets grew and transport in the form of motorcars became more prevalent. But more importantly, tastes changed – couta and salmon were no longer good enough. It was clean white fleshed fish, which was wanted, nothing else. The prize became snapper in due course, a much more difficult fish to catch. Later it was flathead and ling, easier but not as lucrative. Life, as with everything, changed but not for the better, but you had to adapt or die as a fisherman.

Selling the catch had always been quite easy. He would sit with his father on the pier, the local women would politely buy mackerel, salmon and couta. Mackerel was probably the most popular, although they were not particularly fussy, as long as the fish was fresh. It was always fresh, having been caught by him and his father that morning. The impromptu market on the pier meant that they would sell the catch within an hour of coming in. Often, they would not have fish for themselves. No matter, his father would proclaim. He would stop and get some sausages from Ken. Ken the Butcher was a good friend who carried them through a few lean times. Although if the truth be known, his father preferred sausages to fish, in fact he preferred sausages to just about anything.

These days were not that easy. No one came to the pier to buy fish and he had not bothered pulling in to sell fish for many years. People seemed to prefer supermarkets to buy food and not fish at all.

For a while, he had made a living selling fish to the back door of the local pubs and restaurants. But times were changing and there was nothing he could do about it. "Good for curry," he would tell the publican in relation to a fat fresh salmon or mullet. "No one likes curry," the publican would say. One of his customers was Abdul from the local

Indian restaurant. In fact, Abdul was a Lebanese accountant called Fred who had grown up in Warrnambool and then Port Melbourne, but few people knew that. He had taken to wearing a turban and speaking with a thick Indian accent. An accountant by trade, he had presided over his clients' fall into bankruptcy and purchased the business before the taxman knew what had happened.

Apparently, if a family member or partner took a transfer pursuant to a partnership, there was no GST and no stamp duty. The ink on the partnership agreement was still wet when the fees were written off so that he acquired the restaurant. It was better for business if everyone believed he was Pankal's cousin, Abdul, rather than a Lebanese accountant called Fred.

The Fisherman had known Fred since primary school and his secret was safe. Nonetheless, it did not hurt fish sales to remind Fred of school days from time to time.

He had picked up four good size kingfish on the run back to the mooring. Not great money fish but shitloads better than salmon. Fred (Abdul) took them all.

Chapter 5

The old days

His grandfather had also sold fish from a small shed next to the house. His father had too. He had done so for many years after his father died. On Saturdays he would sell fish from the shed. Over the years, the number of people coming to the shop had diminished, such that he did not do either any longer. He relied on taking the fish to the back door of the local restaurants and pubs. The results were good at first but were not that good anymore. Yet it provided an income which he could live on but which required significant frugality.

On moonlit nights and still mornings or afternoons when the birds were close inshore, they would net schools of fish from the beach. They would watch from the headland with binoculars. The great shoals would break off into smaller schools, the big ones were over a thousand tons. The smaller ones maybe five tons. This was the time of spawning, the fish fat and rich with oil, the females full of eggs. They would wait for a calm day, take out the smallest net on the smallest boat and throw a short set, as his grandfather would say. The net would be rowed around the school, quietly, so as not to spook the fish. Although, as his grandfather would say, the fish were hard to spook, they had other things on their minds. All those in the boat would laugh. It was a more relaxed time, rich with family and perhaps a sense of complacency. Things were good, they would always be good.

A long net played out over the back of the dinghy, rowed by one man, played out by another. The first end would be held by several men on shore. The other end grabbed by men at the other end of the beach once the dinghy had been rowed onto shore. Slowly it would be brought in from both ends toward the middle by the men on shore. An old tractor would pull in the net, heavy with fish, onto the beach. The whole school was never taken, only as much as they could sell and smoke over the next few days. The fish were beautiful, shiny green and silver with yellow ringed eyes, fat with oil and eggs. Each one over 3 kg, a big one maybe 5 kg. They would finally drag the flashing, struggling net to the sand to reveal the catch. Everything from mullet, salmon, whiting, stingrays of various types and small gummy sharks would spill, writhing and flipping onto the sand. Swept up into boxes, the catch was quickly sorted and sold to the small crowd of onlookers. The locals would come to the beach on the summer morning or afternoon, depending on when the net was brought in. They would wait and then buy fish on the sand for sixpence a pound, his grandfather would say, double if they were smoked. The fish would be quickly smoked on old wooden beer kegs with driftwood smouldering underneath. The fishermen did a brisk trade. There were good times. Sometimes it was a haul of biblical proportions, a school of mullet or salmon, filling the net to overflowing. A bounty that was rarely seen but eagerly awaited. Such were the days, but such days had not been seen for many decades, as best as he could reckon.

In his grandfather's day the best place to sell fish was at the South Melbourne markets.

Since opening in the late 1860s, the South Melbourne markets had been a bustling place of commerce, specialising in fresh meat, fish, fruit and vegetables. It was the oldest market in Melbourne although, as his grandfather was quick to remind him, had been completely destroyed by fire in 1881. Originally known as the Emerald Hill market but always at the Coventry Street site, his grandfather spoke fondly of it to him. He would speak of taking fish, couta, mackerel and salmon to market by horse and dray. The market was much larger then, he would say, with fish the largest area of all. The fishmongers would display the fish in wooden boxes filled with a mixture of ice and straw. They used chopping blocks like butchers and wore leather aprons speckled with the scales and blood. The market traders were cast from the same mould as each other, all white, mostly Catholic and all as "rough as guts" his grandfather would say. His grandfather would take a load of fish to the market early on market days. On other days he would sell from the pier, the boat moored alongside. His grandfather would weigh the fish using hand scales and wrap them in newspaper. Over the years the market changed, the small sheds were replaced with larger halls and a two-story car park added in the 1970s. The traders changed also. His father would describe them as mostly Greeks running the fish and meat businesses whereas the Italians controlled the fruit and vegetables. This was the state of things from after the Second World War until the 1970s. An influx of Asians, mostly Vietnamese migrants, saw the demographic change slowly, now the fish traders were mostly Asian. Angelo was one of the last of the Greek fishmongers, running a business that his family, one way or another, by cousins, brothers and uncles, had run since the early 1930s. His grandfather would speak of the traders sluicing the chopping blocks and benches with water in wooden buckets, filled from a well. The gutters running to the brim with a mix of scales, fins and blood.

The market was different now, clean and bright, air-conditioned with glass cabinets, shop fronts for each trader. Uniformed attendants weighed fillets of fish on digital scales, carefully wrapping each order three times, paper, plastic and then a paper bag. The latter, a recent concession to aggressive green sensibilities. The clientele had changed too, most dramatically in the Fisherman's time. Previously, the market had been a place for working people to buy fresh, cheap food usually in quite large quantities. Now it was like a big supermarket, populated exclusively by wealthy young professionals with a distinct preference for enviro-friendly greenie politics who must be convinced each product and piece of packaging was good for the fucking planet. The markets had been a place where only local produce was sold, transported the minimum distance and very fresh. It could not be otherwise because the methods of keeping the product cold did not go beyond wet hessian bags in his grandfather's time.

Now the market was full of fish and seafood, each with a description of what it was as well as where it had come from and who had caught it. Scallops from Canada, crab legs from Alaska, lobsters from the USA, halibut from God knows where. The Fisherman did not trade at the markets much these days and had not for many years. Sometimes he would sell a box of premium fish to Angelo but preferred to sell them to Frank at the restaurant from whom he got a better deal. Angelo was making more money selling cray tails from Thursday Island, prawns from the Gulf, Canadian scallops and Long Island lobsters to waste time on a box of snapper from the Bay.

Slackwater

Chapter 6

Boat maintenance, the Bantam and the Handbag

In winter he would take the boat out of the water and park it in the street outside his house. He would strip the hull and recaulk any planks that were leaking. He would then tar the joints between all the planks and scrape them back with the tool his father had made for that purpose. He would paint the hull with hot linseed oil which he heated on the brazier he kept beside him on the street. The same brazier was used to heat the tar to seal the joints between each plank. Then he would paint the hull with an antifouling paint and allow it to dry for a few weeks. It was a time which he liked, even though it meant no income. It reminded him of cold clear winter days with his father as they both tended and maintained the boat. There was no talking between father and son which one might imagine these days. It was a silent and solitary task, despite two people being involved. The only break in the silence was when his father told him to correct something or to redo it – "like this," he would say.

Nonetheless, he felt closer to his father as a result, although he did not know why. Usually his mother would bring tea and teacake for afternoon tea, and tomato sandwiches with mint and sugar for morning tea. They were times which he would always remember.

The problem with Port Melbourne was the neighbours, he thought to himself, watching the young couple across the road wheelbarrowing broken concrete down the driveway and into a big yellow skip. They had been breaking up the concrete in the backyard since they had bought the house about six months ago. Con and Effie had lived there for as long as the Fisherman could remember, Effie resplendent in black for years after Con had died. Con had suffered a fatal heart attack while trying to load a 20 kg lamb to the spit in the backyard one Easter weekend. They roasted the lamb the following weekend at the wake to which the Fisherman had been invited. Greeks certainly knew how to have a wake, he remembered. He had been persuaded to try some of the homemade wine, Greeks can be most insistent in these matters. It didn't taste too bad at the time, but he had felt like shit for days.

The new neighbours were quite nice young kids, despite the woman being a lawyer. The boyfriend, or partner in current language, wasn't a bad bloke. An accountant of some type who seemed to be shit-scared of the girl. She had grown up in Broadmeadows, attended a public school and was determined to ride the social elevator as far as possible. Port Melbourne was affordable, hip and sure to attract good capital gains. He had been educated at a small private school in Mentone and did not seem to have a view about anything in particular. Accountants are like that. She had a job as a corporate counsel with a small customs agent in Fisherman's Bend. He worked as a tax accountant in some practice in St Kilda. "Boutique" was how she described it, whatever the fuck that meant. She explained most of these things to him, having crossed the street to introduce herself soon after moving in. He did his best to keep an appearance of interest, if only slightly. She was of some European ethnic derivative, short, fond of fake blonde hair, red fingernails, designer clothes and high heels. She was like a very small chook, the Fisherman had decided. Puffed up with bright plumage and a lot of attitude. She became The Bantam. The partner wore dull blue suits as accountants are supposed to do. He was like some obligatory item which The Bantam needed, in order to achieve her desired social status. He was The Handbag.

It was a post-modern, new age, organic, nuclear free, GM free, plastic bag free world he told himself. It was a full-time job just keeping up with the lingo let alone fighting it.

Since buying the house they had spent every weekend doing something to it – painting, planting a new garden, cutting down Con's prized olive tree in the front yard and pulling down the perfectly good wire fence on the street frontage. They had ripped out the lemon tree and the grapevine over the carport. A picket fence was coming soon, he had been assured. He was not at all surprised.

The car, a shiny black Mini, was parked on the street while the driveway and backyard were being denuded of concrete. Her scooter, a bright red Italian thing was also in the street. They had an elderly Jack Russell terrier, it had been hers, she explained, since she was 17. The Fisherman hated Jack Russells. The problems came thick and fast after they moved in. She would knock on the door at all hours and especially on the weekend. Often to complain, did he own the brindle dog which

Chapter 6

kept crapping on their nature strip? No, he well knew it belonged to old Henry two doors down, but he did not think it necessary to share it with her. "Never seen that dog before in my life," he said, convincingly.

Usually she knocked on the door just to inform him of something which he really did not need to know. Often these information sessions were commenced and ended with "Just so you know…" The subject matter varied, the arrival of a rubbish skip, the removal of a rubbish skip, the arrival of a stump grinding machine, and so on and so forth. He did his best to look attentive. The Bantam seemed to have an uncontrollable desire to ensure that everyone knew what she was doing and that everyone did what she wanted. He felt sorry for the Handbag, but he quietly got over it. No one likes accountants, and he certainly did not.

Soon enough, and predictably, the Bantam found something substantial to complain about, the boat. The loud knock on the door was the Bantam. He had come to know the knock, it was brash and abrupt, just like its owner. Did he know who owned that rotten old boat which was parked opposite their driveway in the street? It was making it difficult to back the car out of the driveway she complained. "It's my boat," he said, "A Mini Cooper could do a U-turn in the street with the boat parked in it," he pointed out. She seemed to drop down a gear at this point and threw a variety of bylaws and regulations into the conversation. Naturally, he did not give a fuck about local bylaws but politely explained that he had been parking the boat there for 40 years, and his father and grandfather before him. He was about to say the deck needed to be stripped and re-painted and that the boat yard was full so he would do it in the street. However, it was too late, she had exhaled loudly, turned on her high heels, and was already clip-clopping down the path. He closed the door. A few days later Arthur, the elderly parking officer from the council, knocked on the door.

"G'day," he said hesitantly.

"G'day," said the Fisherman.

"Mate, it's about the boat," he started apologetically.

"Is this about that bitch from across the road?" asked the Fisherman.

"We are not at liberty to divulge the sources of our information," said Arthur quoting the script from memory.

"So, it is her, that fucking bitch," snorted the Fisherman.

"Yep," said Arthur, "A nasty piece of work".

"Fucken oath" said the Fisherman.

"Listen mate, can you move it on? Soon?"

"As soon as I have recoated the deck, a few weeks if the weather holds out."

"That seems perfectly reasonable to me," said Arthur.

"How about I give you a "temporary" permit? Free of charge and of unlimited duration," he added.

"Fucking fantastic," said the Fisherman.

"That should fix her," said Arthur, writing the permit on a carbon paper book balanced against the weatherboards on the porch.

"I'll put a copy in the letterbox, mate," he added.

"Arthur, you're a prince among men," said the Fisherman.

"Try telling my wife that," Arthur said morosely over his shoulder as he closed the gate on the footpath.

The Fisherman resolved to make sure the repairs took months and very early the following morning he backed quietly out of the driveway making sure he ran over the silly red scooter. It made a satisfying crunch and a clink of broken glass and plastic under the Kingswood's wheels.

The Bantam did not bother him again. The Fisherman was happy, although he felt a little sorry for the Handbag, until he remembered that he was an accountant. No one likes accountants.

Chapter 7

Port Melbourne

He had lived in Port Melbourne all his life, save for a brief time when he crewed on prawn trawlers in the Gulf of Carpentaria, cray boats in Apollo Bay and on the west coast of Tasmania. He lived in the home which his grandfather had built and which had then been owned by his father. The house was a small weatherboard on a double block with two street frontages. It was now a developer's dream. He was often approached to sell it for a large amount of money. For a time, he had been tempted and for a while he may have had to sell but the body and bag trade had kept it in his hands. At least for now. His father and he had built the large shed on the adjacent block in which to work on Molly. It also had a small room which had been used by his father for many years as a shop selling the catch. In the early days the catch was sold from the pier, but it was easier to have a shop.

The big chest freezers were still used in the shop, although they only held some bait and a few fish these days.

Port Melbourne was originally known as Liardet's Beach, after William Liardet, the first settler in 1839. Only a few kilometres from Melbourne, it is bordered by Hobsons Bay to the south and the Yarra River to the north and west. Originally there were two piers, the Railway Pier and the Town Pier. Both were used to unload ships which sat far out into the Bay. Liardet's Beach became known as Sandridge soon after. In 1893 it officially became known as Port Melbourne. In the 1930s, Station Pier had become the disembarking point for post-war overseas immigrants bound for Melbourne.

By the 1940s, it was a big community, its workforce mostly associated with maritime or manufacturing industries. There were 22 hotels in Port Melbourne by 1946, not a bad achievement at all for an area originally so swampy and undesirable that no one wanted to traverse it.

His grandfather had bought some land near Graham Street and proceeded to build a modest weatherboard home. It was built with the profits of fishing, a good honest job his grandfather would often say.

The home on a double block was walking distance to one of the many local hotels, the Sandridge. Although renamed in the early 1930s, it was known to the locals as the Sandridge.

When the Fisherman was a boy, the suburb was different. The milk was delivered by horse and cart. The milkman running ahead of the horse and cart, picking up the empty bottles and replacing them with full ones. The empty bottles were always lined up outside the front gate. The clip clop of the horse was loud in the silence of the early morning before the birds were awake. The night cart man had ceased his runs down the lane a long time ago, but the Fisherman could still remember the clip clop of the night cart horse in the lane behind the house. The earthy aroma of fresh horse poo was quickly replaced by the deeply uncomfortable odour of the drop toilet. As a boy he would throw handfuls of lime into the lavatory to reduce the odour and to make it more palatable for his mother. Alas, it was a characteristic of Port Melbourne life well into the 1960s and 1970s until the sewerage line was put into all the cottages in his street.

Chapter 8

The House

The house that his grandfather had built was a nice Victorian weatherboard in need of new paint but the adjacent block was empty save for the old shed. His grandfather had bought both blocks and built a house for £50. This was a lot of money in those days he had said. However, the fishing was good and he was making money selling smoked and fresh couta, salmon and some kingfish so he could manage the repayments. The best aspect of the land was that it had two street frontages, Ozone Street in the front and Liadet Street in the rear. It was also walking distance to the beach and, more importantly for the Fisherman, the Sandridge, where his knee had been good enough to walk to the pub.

The location, size and street frontages made it a developer's wet dream. They lost sleep thinking about how many apartments and how much money they would make. Unfortunately for them, the Fisherman had no intention of selling. They would knock on the door in shiny suits and shiny shoes, gelled hair and expensive watches. Unctuous, unpleasant people each and every one of them. They were asked if they could come in, whether he was the owner and did he want to sell. "Top dollar," they would say. "Fuck off," he would say to each of them, closing the door forcefully. He took great pleasure in telling them to fuck off. They seemed to take no offence at this and he could only assume that they were used to it. Indeed, it did not stop them from returning year after year.

The local real estate agent tried also. Reno Rocchielli had been a real estate agent in Port Melbourne for as long as anyone could remember. His father, also Reno, had a fruit shop in Bay Street for many years, now an Internet café. Reno Junior did not want to continue in the fruit and vegetable business having unpacked potatoes, wrapped pieces of watermelon in cling film and emptied the big rubbish bins full of rotting produce since he could walk. He was sick of it, he told Reno Senior. Naturally, this caused some consternation in the Rocchielli household but Reno Junior stuck to his guns and got a job at the local realtor, E.W. Smith and Co. Wilbur Smith was an old school real estate agent. Quietly spoken and conservative, over a career of 50 years in the business, he had sold most of the properties in Port Melbourne at one time or another. He could tell you the last time any house had been sold and the price on each occasion.

He sold the business to Reno many years later on the condition that it stayed as E.W. Smith & Co. Reno agreed, and soon after Wilbur died, named it "Reno Rochielli Real Estate". The name was emblazoned on the shopfront in bright signage with Italian colours. This, he thought, would appeal to the post-war migrant population, which it did. Soon he was very successful and wanted to move into property development as well.

The narrow weatherboard house of the Victorian era, the so-called workers cottages, were everywhere in Port Melbourne. They were no more than 12 or 15 feet wide with a corridor on one side and two rooms on the other. A lean-to or skillion roof at the back housed the kitchen, often the biggest room in the house, heated by a wood fired stove and big enough for a table and chairs. The kitchen was where the meals were prepared, cooked and eaten. The roof was of tongue and groove lining boards, as were the walls.

The front sitting room however had lath and plaster walls, a picture rail and either pressed metal or ornate plaster ceilings. The small cast iron fireplace was set into the wall and was fuelled by smoky, smouldering brown coal. The room had Baltic pine floor, covered by a very nice "China" rug. Small yellowing photographs of long forgotten relatives hung from the picture rail. The ceiling was high enough so that the gas incandescent light did not burn the ceiling, the so-called gas ceilings. The fittings were removed long ago but the pipes were still in the roof space, alongside modern electrical wiring for the single lightbulb that hung from the ceiling rose where the gaslight had once proudly been suspended.

The house was cold as charity in winter and hot as hell in summer. The outhouse, still in use but with a relatively modern toilet, flushing directly into the sewerage line that had been run into the house during his father's time. A source of some pride at that time, a cursed trip now in the bitter cold of winter. However, relocating the toilet to a location inside the house was an expense which he could never rationalise.

Chapter 8

The floors were uneven and sloping, bouncing like trampolines in the middle where the old wooden stumps had long since rotted away. The doors still closed although it did not matter to him living alone as he did. When the roof leaked, as it always did, he repaired it with old rusting corrugated iron from the backyard or with blackjack, the fibrous tar paint from the old tin in the shed. A more recent innovation was a shiny silver tape which had a black bituminous backing which was sticky in warm weather and would adhere to even the rustiest of corrugated iron. It worked best when applied in warm weather but sadly that was the worst time to find the leaks and he did not much care for climbing on the roof to mark the leaks in the cold wet of winter. Mostly he used cheap plastic buckets. He had many of them. In truth, he did not care for material things and was not troubled by slight leaks in the roof. He would repair them now and then as he could when they became inconvenient.

He did not abide cigarette smoking and never had partaken himself. His parents had smoked almost incessantly since he was a child. The acrid smell of cigarettes was always present, the blue clouds wafting through the room. The stale nauseating smell of ashtrays were in every room. His father would make his own cigarettes, rolling them from a pouch of cut tobacco in thin cigarette papers. Sealing them with a brief lick, saliva sticking like glue. Always the same brands, 'Champion', 'Ready Rubbed' in the yellow and red pouch, 'Tallyho' cigarette papers. Nowhere to be found these days but a part of his dim childhood memory.

His mother smoked ready-made cigarettes, always the same brand, never filter tipped and certainly not menthol. The smoking at the pub bothered him dreadfully but he would never complain.

The house had yellow ceilings and a stale cigarette smell that never went away, even after all those years.

He was used to it.

Slackwater

Chapter 9

The milk bar

There was a time when every street had a milk bar, a place where one could buy ice cream, lollies, milk and a few out of date and overpriced groceries. These were the precursors of the 24-hour convenience stores which were now open seven days a week. The milk bars in their day filled the gap between the closing of the supermarkets, 5 pm on weekdays and 12 noon on Saturdays. They existed before Sunday trading. They were an integral part of late night and weekend trade which had not yet been overtaken by the multinational supermarket chains. The small business economy was vibrant and profitable, staffed by mums and dads, maybe the occasional surly son or daughter.

He bought bread and milk from the milk bar at the end of his street. It had been there since the 1970s, providing the basic groceries – milk, bread, tinned soup, ice creams and newspapers. It had been run by a cheery Greek man, the late Nick and his wife Rosa since that time. Nick spoke a little English, Rosa, a little more. They were kindly polite people who were happy to be living in this country, happy to have left a life away from war and poverty.

Rosa ran the milk bar in a side street off Graham Street, on her own after her husband had died many years before. She was a short, stout woman who wore the regulation black dress and cardigan required of a widowed Greek woman. The stock in the milk bar was limited, a few tins of soup, some packets of pasta and some tins of baked beans or spaghetti, but she was busy every day. The bell above the door would signal the entrance of the customer then she had would lever herself out of the recliner chair in the corner, abandon the daytime quiz show and take the money for groceries milk or a newspaper. Rosa gave free lollies to the children, free advice to the adults and lemons to those whom she liked, which was not many. The milk bar derived a modest profit, but it was not how she lived. Like her husband, she was a very good fence or reseller of stolen goods. She could move stolen goods quickly and quietly, both of which were desirable traits in her line of work. After the shop was shut, she would take deliveries to the back door of the house by way of the lane at the side. Nothing large and nothing expensive, but a good steady trade in TVs, VCRs, jewellery and watches. No one knew where she on sold them and no one cared. A few people speculated about her source of stolen goods, whilst there were certainly also a lot of candidates. Her cousin, Con the Greek was a hot favourite amongst those who thought about these things. Con was a shifty, weedy man who seemed to have no obvious source of income. In any event, it certainly helped that Rosa had a large extended family with an almost insatiable desire for stolen electrical goods and jewellery.

In the 1990s, the shop was bought by a Vietnamese family who spoke no English. However, they made themselves part of the community and he still bought bread and milk from the shop, although they could not speak to him at all. He could not abide the supermarkets and could not remember the last time that he visited such a place. He hated them with a passion. The milk bar was a place where he could buy a tin of soup, a container of milk, a loaf of bread, and that was all that he needed. He did not need to stand in a queue at the supermarket. This was especially true after the supermarket decided that we needed to save the planet, one plastic bag at a time. He bought sausages and other meat from Ken the Butcher. Now and then he ate fish, but like most fishermen, he was not especially interested in eating fish.

He had spent a lot of time thinking about having no money. It was a reality on a daily level, how much to spend and how much might be coming in from the next throw of the net, or a run in the tide. The problem was that the fashions for fish had changed and people did not want the fish that they had eaten for generations. But it was impossible to know what would be the next fad fish, the next food craze. He only knew how to catch the fish that swam in the seasons and in the sea. He felt like shouting, "Tell me what to catch, I can catch anything that swims, I just need to know."

The truth of it was that he knew the tastes of his buyers as they used to be, they were old-fashioned – blue mackerel, snapper, flathead, flake and anything else was a bonus. The occasional octopus, some scallops if he dredged at night when the fisheries blokes were not around, some mussels if he could bring himself to snorkel for them or rake them from the pylons, much easier, much easier.

Chapter 9

He lived a life dependent upon the ocean, and at the end of the day, he was happy with that. It did not mean that he did not whinge about it, he certainly did, but only sometimes and then only to the regulars in the bar.

Slackwater

Chapter 10

Risky business

As a young man he would sail or motor to the bottom of the Bay, fishing as he went. He would catch mackerel, salmon and couta. He would drift over the weed and sand, catching squid and whiting. In the icebox full of ice and seawater they would keep cool until he tied up at Rye or Sorrento and sold the fish from the pier. Sailing across the Bay to Queenscliff he would catch whiting and squid. He would sell them on the Queenscliff pier or in the estuary of the river. If there was a free mooring he would stay overnight in the estuary. If not, he would skip over to Quarantine Bay, catching kingfish on the way. A good catch meant he would divert to Portsea pier to sell his catch. The bad catch meant he would stay overnight in Queenscliff and fish the Rip on the tide. It was exciting and fun, all at the same time. He learned his craft in these runs. He knew the Bay like the back of his hand. He knew where the whiting liked to school in the summer mornings; where the big snapper lurked on thunderous afternoons; he followed the schools of salmon knowing that the old snapper were deep beneath the school getting a free feed.

However, fishing that way was a young man's game, especially the run to the Rip. After many years he found that he could not do it anymore. His knee, which had been damaged when a fish box full of ice and fish had slammed into it, ached terribly most days. Even more so when the weather was changing from hot to cold. In recent years he had confined the fishing to the top of the Bay. Fortunately, the fishing had been good, at least after the scallop boats had gone. The other knee still had fragments of Vietnamese shrapnel and hurt badly, although it was hard to tell which knee hurt worse.

He would drift for flathead and, on a moonlit night, catch squid in the bright lights from his boat. Sometimes he would fish the Warmies on the Maribyrnong River at the powerhouse outlet. But the Warmies were crowded with small boats and heavy drinkers. He did not like recreational fishermen or the proximity of other boats. Even so, he could catch good mulloway on the full moon.

The oily fish used to sell well, partly because they were traditional and partly, mostly, because they kept better than the white fish. If refrigeration was an issue, which it often was, oily fish kept for longer. They could also be slightly salted or smoked which helped them keep for longer. However, this tradition was not true these days, everyone wanted white fish, which did not taste like fish and which had no bones. Fuck knows how many times the Fisherman had been asked if it has any bones. "Of course it has fucking bones," he would say. "All fish have fucking bones," he would add.

He would moor the boat against the dark shoreline in Quarantine Bay. The dark hull invisible against the scrub on the shore. The boat would sit quietly in the still water within 20 metres of the raging Rip. The waters of Quarantine Bay are a strange, still pond, contrasting with the treacherous Rip. For 150 years it was a mooring place for boats suspected of bringing fevers and other bad conditions; sailors spending their time drinking and throwing bottles into the calm, shallow water. In modern times, the search for empty bottles in the sand had been a drawcard for scuba divers and archaeologists alike. He turned off all navigation lights and watched the big container boat push through the turbulent waters, throwing a white wave at its bow, "A bone in its teeth," his father used to say. The bright orange pilot boat would follow in its wake, until cutting quickly off to starboard towards Queenscliff. This blocked any sight of the man throwing the parcel with a dull coloured float from the port side towards the waiting Fisherman. The pilot could later pick up a small envelope from the front bar of the Queenscliff hotel. His father had done it and his grandfather before him. He had gone with his father a few times when he was getting too old to run the boat by himself.

Yanni the Greek, or latterly, Syd the Squid, would say to him in the bar, "… might be a trip soon, if you're interested?" His father would say, "… might be interested, when?" … next Wednesday?", "Body or bag?". The reference was either to a refugee or a bag heaved overboard with a float. He preferred bags. Bodies were always difficult, half drowned, frozen and he was wary of them as they were capable of anything. All were desperate stowaways, refugees or sailors wanting a better life or trying to escape a worse one. Either way they went into a small space under the floor in the forecastle of the boat. In the same small compartment was his father's 303 rifle, wrapped in oilskin and covered in machine oil to prevent rust.

Chapter 11

A morning fishing

The next fish was the same as the one before. So too was the one after that. The diesel throbbed quietly as the old windlass groaned as it brought in the net. He snapped the spine of each fish as he had done with the first. The net made a dull scraping sound as it came in over the gunwale.

"Fucking salmon," he said quietly to himself. The water lapped quietly at the side of the boat. He tossed each lifeless fish into the wooden box under the transom. He shook the box occasionally to settle the fish into the ice. Every three or four metres, as the net came in, there was another fish or two, or not as the case may be. The fish came in, limp and lifeless, big eyed in death. Sometimes salmon, sometimes mackerel, often mullet. His reaction to each was the same, quiet disappointment. His was more sanguine these days than he had been in his youth, when the money meant more than it did these days, although in many ways the money was more important now that there was less of it. Each fish was different, each beautiful in its own way, although he no longer saw the beauty of the animal.

Nonetheless, the salmon were sparkling when they came in on the net, silver green with speckled flanks and yellow eyes, each of about 2 kg in weight. Beautiful, even in death, but they had no market value these days.

"Fucking salmon," he would say to himself. The mackerel were resplendent in silver and blue, with flanks painted in various tones of aqua and darker stripes to camouflage them from predators. Each was like a rocket underwater, a silver flash in the blue green water, invisible to anyone above. White bellies reflecting the grey sky, a ghost to the enemy below. Sadly, they were not smart enough to avoid the net, silent and invisible in the deep. The mullet were surface fish who liked the shallower waters, silver sided with deep yellow ringed eyes. Placid vegetarians who blundered into the nets softly as was their habit but could never escape. Such was their watery grave, as was that of their cousins, the salmon, the mackerel and so many others. The garfish and the snapper seemed altogether too smart to be caught, such was his luck.

Nonetheless, he set the nets seeking garfish and snapper. Rarely was he successful but always optimistic. A fisherman must be optimistic.

"Fucking mullet," he said. He had retrieved the net and brought in nothing but salmon, save for a few mullet and quite a lot of mackerel. In the past, good catches of salmon would have meant a modest profit for the trip. Now it would not break even, certainly not with mackerel and mullet. The boat rocked slightly in the early light, the sun now over the horizon in an increasing display of ruby red, orange and yellow. The sky went from black to blue with the stars retreating over the horizon. The elegant moment of dawn quickly faded into the more prosaic morning. He missed the dawn almost as soon as it had arrived, so fleeting was its presence. A few barracouta, "nasty bony good for nothing bastards," the Fisherman called them. They were tossed into the bilge having no other use than bait these days. He had set the net in the early morning, coal black and silent. At this time of year, it was cold without being bitter and the wind was gentle unlike its evil counterpart in winter. These were the good days insofar as the weather was concerned. The fishing was another matter however, so vastly different from when he had finished with his father or fleetingly with his grandfather.

Nonetheless, the routine of launching the boat, setting the net, hauling and sorting remained ever present. Such was the life of a fisherman, even today. He pulled in the handlines, which he had earlier set with pilchards and squid for any big snapper on the reef below. The hooks were empty, as usual.

By the time the sun had broken free of the water and become a red ball on the horizon, he had hauled in the net. He coiled the lines and packed the net carefully. He set a course for home. He did it without thinking or using a compass. He knew the direction home like he knew his way around his house in the dark. The water was his home, different to the land, but his home, nonetheless. A kingfish or two would help, he hoped they might be around in the warmer water at this time of year. The lures dragged the lines over the transom and out well away from the wash of the boat, deep into the mid-water. They were rigged with his grandfather's big brass swivels to keep the heavy lines from twisting and untangling, homemade stainless-steel wire traces to stop the sharp teeth from cutting the line. Sparkling, flashing, setting a dance irresistible to the fish, if they were there. He added a few handmade lures, made like

Chapter 11

his grandfather had shown him. Silver foil wrapped tightly around a long-shanked hook, a brightly coloured bead and a chook feather for extra shine and twirl. He looped a piece of rope over the tiller. The boat would find its own way home.

He turned to the fish in the box, a box made by his grandfather and used by his grandfather for 35 years, then his father and now by him. Dark with fish blood and slime, bleached on the edges. The blood, scales and slime drained through the wooden slats on the bottom and sides. Oily fish such as salmon, mackerel and mullet needed to be bled quickly or the flesh would spoil. He went to work cutting and bleeding each fish. He worked quietly and efficiently, his hands working automatically with the muscle memory born of decades of practice. The gulls were awake by now, following the boat hoping for a free feed. They would not be disappointed as he tossed the guts into the wake of the boat. It was not his intention to feed the gulls but rather to encourage the fish to come up and then become interested in the lures. The only good use for salmon, he thought to himself, was feeding the birds. Nonetheless, he treated the fish respectfully as he would any animal which he had killed. He slid them into the ice and saltwater slowly in order to keep them pristine until he could refrigerate them properly.

By this time the dolphins were awake and looking for breakfast. The Fisherman always looked forward to them, although most fishermen took a different view. He spoke to them as individuals whom he had come to know over the years. He kept a few smaller fish for them, whole and not gutted. He knew they would not eat either gutted fish or even the entrails. The dolphin twittered, thanking him for the fish and were gone as quickly as they had come. He was sad to see them go but knew they would come back next time.

He liked to think the dolphins were seeking companionship and saying thank you for the fish. However, he suspected they were saying "fuck you, we already ate the best ones". He did not care either way, they were a welcome distraction in the cold dawn and on the long run home. He kept the nice garfish for breakfast and a nice fat mullet for dinner. They were only worth a few dollars, but he knew that they were the best of the day's catch

Slackwater

Chapter 12

The Pub

The pub was built in the late 1800s in the grand Victorian style popular for such buildings at the time. At one time a centre of the local working community it was now something of an anomaly, the workers having long since left. The surrounding streets were still replete with workers cottages usually with descendants of the original owners still in residence. However, such were the times that the pub's traditional clientele had shrunk to about almost negligible numbers.

The publican's name was Bill, Bill the Younger or Young Bill to the old blokes. It had been his father's pub and after Old Bill died (he was named after his father) it was taken over by Young Bill. He had not been young for a very long time but most of the men in the front bar still called him Young Bill. It was probably appropriate Young Bill thought, because they had all known Bill (Old Bill) and were all older than he was. Nonetheless, it did get up his nose now and then.

Bill had taken over the pub in the early 1960s, a very good time to own a pub in Port Melbourne. There were no drink driving laws, the locals were heavy drinkers, beer was cheap to buy and profitable to sell. Best of all the police were friendly. He had been to school or played football with most of them and no one expected fancy food at the pub. Life was good and so were the profits.

Old Bill had bought the freehold from the brewery in the 1930s when Port Melbourne was in decline and no one wanted to run a pub in Port Melbourne. The brewery and others had tried to buy it back many times. Young Bill had been offered huge sums to sell. He enjoyed telling them to fuck off. But he knew that selling it was inevitable as he had no children and no one to pass it on to. His wife, Cheryl, had run off with Gary, a used car salesman from Sandringham. Recently divorced, she now lived in Brighton with two poodles and an endless supply of New Zealand Sauvignon Blanc. Serves her right, Young Bill thought to himself. He never liked Gary much but after Cheryl left him, he almost felt sorry for Gary. Almost but not quite.

Young Bill yearned for the old days when the pub was busy every night until closing and all day Saturday. It was a place where you could buy cheap whitegoods and vacuum cleaners. Televisions also on occasion. It was amazing how many shipping containers were damaged on the waterfront and the contents spilled into the sea, gone forever only to resurface in their original packaging in the car park of the pub late at night. The boys from the Painters and Dockers, the local stevedores knew nothing about it. Curious really.

Young Bill would sometimes buy fish from the Fisherman. Naturally, Young Bill wanted white fish, but the Fisherman did not have it to sell very often these days. Young Bill would buy gummy shark if it was on offer. He would tell the diners that it was flathead. When the diners were yuppies, whom he despised, he would tell them it was snapper. They always believed him. "You don't get wood ducks every day," he would say. "You have to enjoy them when you do," he would croak, retelling the story to the public bar. Scallops were a favourite of his. He would use a scone cutter to cut nice round pieces from stingray wings which the Fisherman had brought him. He would say, "The bastards will never know the difference," and they didn't.

As the Fisherman's father would often say, "Young Bill is as crooked as a dog's hind leg." Whilst this was undoubtedly true, Young Bill was a decent bloke and everyone quite liked him. However, they did not like his collection of hula shirts or the bad toupee he had taken to wearing.

After mooring the boat, the Fisherman rowed ashore in the tender. He loaded the box of fish into the old Holden station wagon and set off to sell it.

He arrived at the pub too early to be open but he knew that Young Bill would be in the kitchen. Young Bill lived upstairs and would come down early to make a healthy breakfast of bacon, eggs, sausages and baked beans every morning. It was the one thing that he could cook properly. "G'day mate," he said as the Fisherman entered the kitchen. "How about breakfast?" "Not hungry," said the Fisherman, after a quick glance at the plate. "It's the only thing I can cook," said Young Bill. "I know," said the Fisherman. "Just had some breakfast," he said, determined not to get trapped.

Chapter 12

"Fancy a box of fish?" he enquired. "Snapper?" asked Young Bill. "Salmon and mullet," said the Fisherman. "Good for curry." "No one likes fish curry here," replied Young Bill. The Fisherman was keeping the snapper and gurnard for the cafe down the road. He quite liked Maria, the Italian woman who owned it. It would be wrong to say he had intention in Maria's direction, but he did think that she was a very pleasant woman.

"No worries," the Fisherman said. "See you later for a beer." "Right," said Young Bill, his mouth full of overcooked egg and burnt sausages. A local Indian restaurant, 'The Raj', was a few streets away. It was a place for dodgy curry and fresh gastro. He had often sold dodgy fish to the owner, Gupta. In fact, Gupta's real name was Muhammad. Muhammad was from Afghanistan and did not know much about Indian cooking, but Indian food was more popular than Afghan. The food at 'The Raj' was about as authentic as Muhammad. Muhammad cooked from a Woman's Weekly Indian cookbook he had found at the local opportunity shop.

Muhammad had taken to wearing a turban and speaking with a thick Indian accent. At several times during the year, he painted a red dot on his forehead. The locals mostly knew that Muhammad was Lebanese and didn't eat much Indian from 'The Raj'. It was better that way.

Muhammad was as shifty as a shithouse rat when it came to commercial dealings but he was interested in the fish. The Fisherman knew that because Muhammad looked in the box and said, "What do you want for that shit?" This, of course, meant that he knew it was fish but also, he knew that they were not premium fish. He also figured that no one else would by them.

"10 a kilo for the lot," said the Fisherman.

"Fuck that," said Muhammad, all pretence of an Indian accent gone. "$25 for the lot. No one else will buy them." They settled on $40, barely enough to pay for fuel and bait. As usual, Muhammad got the better deal, but the fish needed to be moved quickly.

"Any smarter and you would wear underpants outside your trousers you prick," said the Fisherman.

"Fuck you," said Muhammad over his shoulder, lugging the fish into the kitchen.

The few remaining salmon were given to Oleg the Russian who lived across the road. Oleg quite liked salmon, smoking them on his Weber and eating them cold with vodka or beer and mustard. It must be a Russian thing, the Fisherman decided after trying the smoked fish smeared in mustard one day. He did not mind the vodka though.

Chapter 13

The regulars

The bar was usually quiet and sparsely populated. It was the type of bar where everyone turned to see who was walking in. They expected to know the entrant and were rarely disappointed. When a stranger entered the room it would become noticeably quieter. Usually the stranger would leave reasonably quickly.

Once some yuppies in pink polo shirts wandered into the bar. Young Bill eyed them frostily.

"Two Coronas mate," one said.

"Don't have any," said Young Bill.

"Two Carltons then," then said the other.

"Lines are all down," said Young Bill, filling a glass for Errol.

"Doesn't look like it," said the first.

"Well they fucking well are," said Young Bill.

"What's that," asked the other, pointing at the expertly poured beer. "A fucking ham sandwich?" asked the Yuppie.

"Fuck off dickhead," growled Young Bill.

The yuppies promptly exited, no doubt to find the Mexican beer and tapas in Graham Street to their satisfaction. Young Bill was getting less hospitable in his old age.

"What was wrong with them?" asked Errol.

"I hate yuppies," said Young Bill.

"Fuckers," said Errol.

Errol, a former painter and docker was 93 years old, had cataracts in both eyes, not many teeth and could barely walk. He lived a few doors away and would shuffle into the pub every day at 11.00 a.m. Young Bill would help him home about 3.00 p.m., often taking him a toasted sandwich for dinner. It was the least that Young Bill could do. Errol had been a regular at the pub for over fifty years.

Also, Young Bill owed Errol a favour or two. Errol had run a garden supply business, specialising in compost which he sold at a good profit to the good people of Brighton and South Melbourne. They couldn't get enough of it. Errol prepared the mulch using a mulcher he had made with a turbo charged diesel motor from an old Kenworth prime mover. The truck had been written off by the insurers after a rather nasty accident. Errol took the insurance money, repurposed the motor and gave the truck a nice new life on the Sunshine Coast with new VIN numbers. It was a win-win, he would often say.

In any event, Errol could mulch anything using his Kenworth powered mulcher, even the dog of the bloke whom Young Bill's wife had run off with. Young Bill did not forget that sort of thing. He looked after Errol.

Errol always sat next to Phil, a youngster of 78 years. Phil, or Fabulous Phil, liked sharp clothes and gold jewellery. His few remaining strands of hair were painstakingly smoothed over his bald skull. Fabulous Phil had been a car salesman for over 50 years. "Phil's Motors" was a Port Melbourne institution, no car had ever done more than 50,000 miles or 100,000 kms or so the odometer said. Variously described as being as crooked as a dog's hind leg or couldn't lie straight in bed, Phil liked buying a round of drinks.

Everyone tolerated him, even his perfect shiny white false teeth. "You would have to count your fingers after shaking his hand," they would say, but not a bad bloke they all agreed. "Just never buy a car from him," Errol would add.

Phil had been born in Manchester and suffered from an English accent and a stammer. Whilst both were apparently unrelated, he tried to speak as little as possible and with a broad Australian accent in order to better sell cars. The result was that his conversation was often limited to "fuckenoath" or "fuckyeah". The clientele of the pub did not seem to mind his limited conversational skills. In truth, they found it rather acceptable that he just agreed with most things. Phil decided it was time to retire after a nasty run in with Irek the Albanian, a rather nasty fellow with a lot of gold fillings in his teeth. Whilst it was a minor matter involving the provenance of a car and, in particular, its engine, Irek seemed to take it rather personally. Phil decided that he disliked car bombs intensely but was rather relieved when the insurance company paid him the inflated value on the cars, including the two extra burned out wrecks which he added later. Rather than look a gift horse in the mouth and deciding that you only get one Irek in your life, Phil promptly retired.

Errol agreed with Phil's career decision and in particular his assessment of Irek's character and disposition "M-m-m-mean at both ends and n-n-n-nasty in the m-m-m-middle," said Phil in a rare exposition. "Fucker," said Errol.

Phil was in the bar most days and was happy to be there. Although he did get uncomfortable when strangers in suits came to visit looking for Oleg. He remembered what Young Bill had said one day about no statute of limitations for fraud. Phil preferred the quiet life as long as it did not involve jail for insurance fraud.

The other full-time resident in the bar was Cliff. In fact, Cliff was a full-time resident in the pub, having lived in a room upstairs for as long as anyone could remember. Cliff was small and wiry with more tattoos than you could poke a stick at. Cliff had been a worker all of his life in various occupations, always outdoors. A stevedore, a truck driver, a stockman, and latterly a council worker fixing the roads. He had no family but befriended Young Bill and in return for room and board attended to the various chores which needed doing around the pub. He was also a good handyman, if it couldn't be fixed with a screw or some Araldite it couldn't be fixed, he was fond of saying. Like most men of his generation his conversation was limited and peppered with cockney slang. "Boat race" or "dial" was a "face", "plate of meat" was a reference to "feet" and so on. The locals could understand him, but sometimes when he got excited, subtitles would have been of assistance.

Cliff sometimes did other jobs for Bill the Younger, which were best left unsaid.

Slackwater

Chapter 14

Oleg the Russian

Oleg the Russian came to Australia to work on the Snowy Mountains Scheme. He stayed after the project was finished. He moved to Melbourne and went underground. Visas were not a big thing then and Oleg just knew how to slip under the radar. Oleg had never paid tax and had never voted. However, he did think that Australia was a good place to live. "A fucking great country," he would say in a thick accent. In fact, his name was not Oleg and he was not Russian. He came from Kazakhstan before it was a country that anyone had heard of. He called himself Oleg, it was as good a name as any. A regular at the pub he was known as Oleg the Russian for obvious reasons. More of this later.

Oleg hated anyone with left wing political views. "Fucking communists," he would say. Unfortunately for Oleg, Port Melbourne was a socialist stronghold, currently in love with the Greens. At one point, Oleg had apparently done a disservice by some Norwegians. As a consequence, his greatest condemnation was to describe someone as a "Fucking Norwegian". He had a way of saying it which conveyed a deep hatred. He was about 5'7" in height, neither young nor old, lean but not over muscled with a face that had seen a hundred icy dawns. Oleg was a man that people did not look twice at but if they did were not at all sure he was friendly. In fact, Oleg was not friendly. Oleg loved to hate. He hated better than anyone the Fisherman had ever met.

Once the Fisherman glimpsed a large tattoo on Oleg's chest. It was military in style, with a shield, a knife and some Russian words. He asked Oleg what it meant. "I forget," said Oleg darkly, buttoning his shirt. Another time the Fisherman asked him about the tattoo again. "My mother," said Oleg. "That's nice," said the Fisherman. He did not ask again and noticed how Oleg kept the tattoo out of plain sight, even on a hot day buttoning up his shirt to the neck.

Oleg kept to himself but did like the front bar of the pub, where he would spend most afternoons. He had a job as a cleaner at the local school which he did at night. Oleg liked working at night, no one asked him any questions and he did not have to tell them any lies.

He sat in the same place at the end of the bar, nursing a beer and reading, apparently Russian novels tucked behind the form guide. The stool he preferred kept his back to the wall and gave him plain view of the two entrances into the bar. The locals did not notice this strategic placement until after the incident in the bar.

In the early days, until the locals knew he would only sit in that place, he would enter and leave the bar if it was occupied. Soon it became his stool, never occupied by anyone else. For a while, men in cheap suits would come to the bar and ask if anyone knew a bloke called Vasily Tepelov. Everyone in the bar would give the question long consideration and solemnly answer, "No, never heard of him" or "Is he that tennis player bloke?" Oleg would sit quietly in the corner, studying the form guide. When asked he too would say no, he had never heard of any Vasily bloke, in his best Australian accent. The men in cheap suits would leave. They returned several times over the next few months and then gave up. No one ever asked Oleg why they were looking for him, but the common theory was that they were from the migration department or the tax office or both. It did not really matter which. For his part, Oleg never mentioned why the men may have been visiting the pub, if indeed they had been looking for him at all.v

Chapter 15

The bar

The front bar was on the corner with a door which opened straight into the main bar. The door was one of those split doors with a spring on each side. The springs were strong and the doors narrow. A challenge for the patrons entering, certainly upon leaving, many had fallen foul of the doors, questioning the publican's heritage as they did. The publican did not care. They always returned.

The bar was made of timber and roughly "U" shaped. It had footrests, a place where the spittoon used to be and a separate space where the ashtrays used to be. Brass coat hangers were under the outside edge of the bar so a man could take off his jacket for some serious drinking. The carpet was dark, shiny and sticky in places, just like pub carpet should be. The beer taps were crystalline with ice, each looking like a marble column. The beer taps had coloured labels denoting the brands. The brands were old, this was no place for so-called craft beers. Accordingly, there were only a few taps, each well-known, well used and well loved. Beer branded towels, rubber backed, were scattered on the bar. Each performed a function, covering the scars, dents, scratches and chipped lacquer of the surface.

A few high tables were scattered in the room with correspondingly high stools. Each stool was finished in worn black vinyl, legs in chipped black paint, crossbars polished back to bare metal by boots and shoes over the years. The sky-blue "CUB" clock read 11:57, as it had done for as long as anyone could remember. The fireplace was as old as the pub but still worked. It provided hearty warmth in winter, mallee roots smouldering quietly from opening until closing.

A blackboard menu occupied one wall, written in a curling longhand long ago. The food unchanged since it had been first written and the prices, mostly remaining the same, notwithstanding the complaints of the regulars. The menu was predictable and of small compass. Steak, a burger, chicken parma, tripe, lambs fry (with bacon) and sausages with mash. The specials were not all that special, but the term was applied to items which were not available every day. Yet each were from the same song book: corned beef, liver and onions, and maybe steak and kidney pie. The publican tried to add Thai green chicken curry. It lasted about one week. Naturally, a pie warmer sat on one end of the bar. Pies, sausage rolls (no vegetarian ones) were added every morning fresh from the freezer. A glass case with sandwiches was adjacent to the pie warmer. White bread ham and onion sandwiches, made by the publican, sat on white plates covered in cling film.

Mustard yellow ceiling tiles were a testament to decades of smoking in the bar and contributed a faint ash smell which never quite went away. A football tipping board hung on one wall. The regulars' names alongside the predicted victory of tribal contests in the forthcoming season. For a time, the publican had encouraged business with a meat raffle on a Thursday night. A tray piled high with chops, sausages, mince, tripe and kidneys would change hands for a 50 cent ticket. Those days were long gone, such was the lack of custom of the pub.

The narrow room adjacent to the public bar was formerly the ladies lounge. The frosted door between the bar in the lounge was long gone. However, the servery style opening between the bar and the lounge remained. It was a servery of sorts in the days when the ladies lounge was in use, but its real function was to enable the ladies, so-called, to keep an eye on things in the bar. They would whisper to the barman that it was quite "time", although he would ignore them. Thereafter, they would screech through the servery and the husband would come to heel. Such is married life. The ladies lounge had not been the ladies lounge for decades, a good thing the permanent residents of the bar would often say.

Bill hated the Graham Street bypass with the same passion that he had for Collingwood. "That fucking bridge" or "That damned overpass" or just "That fucking thing" were the only ways he would describe it, never by name. This was quite understandable because Bill considered that the Graham Street overpass had killed his business. In fact, the overpass had been the straw that the dying camel's back had not needed, but there was no denying that the camel was very unwell at the time. The Graham Street overpass was built in the late 1970s after the Westgate Bridge was finished. It was considered that the bridge would increase traffic through Port Melbourne to get to the bridge. Whether it did or not, Bill considered it was an abomination that took his pub, from a visible reasonably busy location to a hidden backwater, virtually under the shadows of the overpass. The fact that the Foresters Arms hotel across the road was demolished did nothing to appease Bill. He considered that it made the offence even worse. Graham Street station was on the Port Melbourne train line, originally known as the Sandridge line. It was opened in 1854 by the Melbourne and Hobson's Bay Railway Company to carry passengers and freight to and from Station Pier. The overpass was thought also to improve the flow of traffic by removing the boom gates on Graham Street which were often closed due to the passage of trains. The problem was that the road traffic never came through Port Melbourne and the Port Melbourne line was closed in 1987 when the St Kilda line was completed. Nonetheless, the regulars considered it was a good result.

The regulars would listen to Bill's rants which occurred with monotonous regularity. They would nod and say "Fuckers", "Shit yeah" and "Arseholes" when the opportunity arose. In truth, they were all quite happy with the current arrangement, it made the Sandridge their own private club, no newcomers allowed. It also meant that the pub did not shake and vibrate when the heavy trucks roared past like in the old days. It was much better, all things considered, so far as the patrons were concerned. They never told Bill their views on the subject however.

Bill the Younger was always looking for ways to improve the pub business. He had tried cheap beer, topless barmaids, raffles and bingo but was currently convinced that up-market food would be the answer.

"A gastropub, that's the thing," he announced.

"What?" asked Errol.

"Modern Australian food with a fusion element," Bill quoted from a restaurant review. "That's what everyone wants."

"What the fuck is that?" asked Phil.

"Fucked if I know," said Bill, "But I've got to get some."

"The only thing that you would get in this place is gastro," said Phil. "It's been a gastropub for a long time."

"Get fucked," said Bill.

"Fffuckenoath," said Phil.

Slackwater

Chapter 16

The food in the pub

Like most working-class suburbs in Melbourne, Port Melbourne was replete with pubs in the 1800s. Every corner, especially near the railway stations, was occupied by a hotel, always two stories high. Eating and drinking below, accommodation above, a good design really.

The hotel was the focus of society for many people in their heyday, providing social interaction as well as cheap food and drink for working men and women. Pubs were also very profitable for their owners; beer was cheap to make and sold for a very good mark up. Various factors combined to erode the place of the hotel in society. Television, packaged alcohol, and latterly, drink-driving laws to mention a few.

The Fisherman's grandfather and father had always attended the Sandridge, mostly because it was walking distance from the house. So too, he attended the Sandridge although he mostly drove because of his bad knees. Sadly, the pubs were disappearing before his eyes. Almost literally. The London, a magnificent two-story Victorian at the end of the pier had fallen into disrepair after the wharves had moved up the Yarra. It was now long gone. The Fountain Inn on Raglan Street was still there but now rebadged as a yuppie watering hole. The Pier in Bay Street, built on the site of one of the first hotels of the same name was also gone. Built by Liardet himself, a significant loss. The list went on, the Flower now a wine bar, the Sandridge (one of two of the same name), formerly the Freemasons Tavern, the Builders Arms, the Hibernian, all long gone. The Iberian was now an Indian restaurant, on the corner of Graham and Ross Streets.

"We are almost the last one," lamented Bill the Younger. "All the others have gone, the Hibernian, the Freemasons, the London… too many to mention. A complete fucking shame," said Bill.

"Don't forget the Builders Arms and The Swallow," added Errol.

"We are a fucking endangered species," said Phil.

"Yeah," said Errol.

"Shit yeah," said Bill. "It is up to us to keep our traditional customs and practices alive, to preserve our habitat values," he added.

"What the fuck is he talking about?" asked Phil.

"Fucked if I know," said Errol.

As they were arguing, Helen the skinny girl from next door came through the pub door. Towel over her shoulder and smiling brightly she waved to Bill and said, "Good morning". She skirted around the bar and skipped up the stairs. Helen was a girl from the country who lived in the old butcher shop next door. She had converted it into a one-bedroom flat but did not have a shower. Bill felt sorry for her and let her use the shower upstairs in the pub. She was a student who kept to herself, occasionally sitting in the corner of the bar reading a thick book and making notes, sipping a lime and soda. She was no trouble and most of all she was nice to Errol, who adored her.

For a long time, the pub had offered food. All pubs offered cheap basic food. It was a way to move the beer and they virtually gave away the food in the old days. For some time, the menu on the wall had two sections. Pub classics and specials. Classics were not really classics, but they were reliable – chicken parmigiana, mixed grill, steak, fish and chips and the burger. The specials were not so special and best left alone. In fact, the same could be said of the classics. However, for a long time it was a place where, if you were in the know, and the clientele was, you could get good reliable food for not much money. Monday was $10 steak day, Tuesday was $10 beef casserole and rice, Wednesday was $10 roast with everything, Thursday was $10 spaghetti and meatballs, Friday was meat tray raffle day. "What more could you ask for?", the publican would say. No one would disagree.

These days were different. Bill the Younger had pies in the warmer and he had the sandwich toaster. The latter was relatively new, the former had been on the bar for as long as anyone could remember. Insofar as sandwiches were concerned, the patrons would say they wanted a sandwich or one of those new ones. The latter was toasted, the former was not. But mostly they would have a pie. Chips were a recent thing, these 'frozen-in-the-oven-cooked' variety. They were quite happy with them, they were soft and did not fuck up their false teeth. However, if they were cooked crisp as they should be, the patrons complained loudly. Steak sandwiches were good but these days they found them a bit hard to eat. It was the sort of bar where everyone turned around

Chapter 16

when you walked in. If they did not know you the frost in the air was palpable. The problem was that you had to walk in the door for at least 10 years before they considered that they knew you. It was that sort of place. They liked it that way and the truth of it was that Bill the Younger did too. He just would not admit it.

Bill the Younger tried a local bloke as the chef for a while. The 'chef' told them it was food like mum used to make. The locals said if mum had cooked like this that they would have moved out or died trying. Then there was an Italian bloke who cooked at the pub on Thursdays and Saturdays. The dishes were good said the regulars but too much garlic they said. "Get rid of the garlic and serve it with gravy and it would be okay," they said. Later, Bill tried a Greek fellow, but he would only cook lamb, mostly souvlakia. The locals did not like lamb unless it came with mint sauce, peas, gravy and roast potatoes. The next was a Burmese chap who said that he grew up in Abbotsford and barracked for Collingwood. Bill the Younger thought that was most unlikely given his broken English, but he cooked chook parmas, liver and onions and the other stuff that the clientele expected. It all went very well until the blokes from the Immigration Department visited the pub one day. The Burmese cook was out the back door and over the back fence before anyone could say Jack Robinson (in Burmese), certainly before anyone knew that he had gone. A couple of smouldering chook parmas in the deep fryer was the only sign that he had been there.

The music in the pub was rolled gold from the '70s and '80s – INXS, the Pretenders, Queen, the Rolling Stones and the like. Occasionally it went to the '60s – Ella Fitzgerald, Nina Simone and Duke Ellington. The bar occupants would nod and smile slightly when they heard a song that they knew. They would complain loudly if the music was modern or headbanging, whatever that meant.

They were constant in their time warp, the bar that time forgot. Every day was a day from the top 10 of some year. As long as it had a 1970s or a 1980s date in front of it, they did not really care.

Slackwater

Chapter 17

Body or bag

The engine was running rough, coughing and spluttering all the way back to the mooring. He tried stopping and starting, clearing the fuel line but nothing made any difference. The power was there one minute and gone the next. In fact, this had been occurring for some time, but he had not wanted to acknowledge it.

"How much?" he said to Yanni the mechanic.

"It needs a new crankcase," said Yanni.

"It'll be okay just change the spark plugs and the oil," said the Fisherman.

"No, it won't be I've been telling you that for two years," said Yanni. "It needs a new crankcase."

"How much?" asked the Fisherman.

"I don't know… They haven't made these things for 50 years," said Yanni. "$5,000," he added.

"If you don't know how much it is going to cost then how do you know it is going to cost $5,000?" asked the Fisherman.

"Well, that is the price," said Yanni. "And by the way, you still owe me for last time."

"Well, last time was too much," said the Fisherman.

"I can use the crankcase from a Datsun 180Y… Not later than 1974," said Yanni. "Go to the Datsun wreckers in Dandenong, ask for Mick, he will give you what I need, tell him that I sent you," said Yanni.

"Fuck," said the Fisherman.

"Do you want this or not?" asked Yanni, "Just do it," said the Fisherman.

"Fuck," added the Fisherman.

"Don't forget the dry rot," said Yanni.

"What dry rot?" asked the Fisherman.

"Don't pretend that I haven't told you," said Yanni. "Most of the keel is fucked."

"How much?" asked the Fisherman.

"$5,000," said Yanni.

"What is it with you and $5,000?" asked the Fisherman.

"That is the price, for anyone else it would be a shitload more," said Yanni.

"Fuck," said the Fisherman.

"Do you want it or not?" asked Yanni.

"Yes, just fucking do it," said the Fisherman.

"Fuck," he said again as he left.

The thing that he was most upset about was not the price of the crankcase, which he knew he had to fix, or the dry rot which he had known about for years, but that he would need to see Syd the Squid.

Sydney Goldblatt was a local accountant, thoroughly Jewish. Sydney decided it was better for business if he gave his firm an Anglo-Saxon name – Churchill and Partners. It did not matter to him that there was and never had been a Churchill in the business, or any partners for that matter. Indeed, he would happily answer to Mr Churchill if clients addressed him as such. Sydney was also a private mortgage broker, although some may have more aptly described him as a loan shark. Indeed, the local magistrate had described him as such on several published occasions. It was a description that Sydney found quite hurtful. He saw himself as a community resource much like a bank. Except banks did not send Ken the Butcher around to see you if you were late in paying. Sydney was widely known as Syd the Squid, although not to his face.

He had not gone to see Syd for many years. He did not like seeing Syd the Squid. The runs down the Bay for a body or bag were something that he had more or less said to himself that he would never do again. But he knew this time that he had no choice.

"Body or bag," he asked quietly, slowly rotating the glass of beer on the shiny wooden bar of the Imperial.

"Bag," said Syd the Squid, talking into his tonic water.

The police car, siren screeching loudly went past the pub, drowning out Syd the Squids reply. "What?" asked the Fisherman.

"Fucking bag," he hissed, glancing down the bar.

Chapter 17

"All right," said the Fisherman indignantly. "Didn't hear you."

"Not something I want to say out loud," said Syd, through gritted teeth. "Usual fee," he added.

"The price is ten grand," said the Fisherman.

"Ten grand," said Syd incredulously. "It has never been ten grand."

"Well, it is now," said the Fisherman. "The boat needs fixing," he added.

"Let me guess, that prick Yanni wants ten large to fix the boat," sneered Syd. He did a lot of sneering. He was good at it.

"He is a good mechanic," said the Fisherman.

"He couldn't lie straight in bed," said Syd, which was a big call from Syd, one of the shiftiest blokes the Fisherman had ever met.

"Let me guess, he sent you to the Datsun wreckers in Dandenong to get the parts,' said Syd the Squid.

"How did you know that?" asked the Fisherman.

"It is owned by his cousin, Mustafa, another shifty prick," said Syd the Squid.

"He is a good mechanic," said the Fisherman again.

"Go to Yoshi, he will fix it for you," said Syd. Yoshi was Syd's second cousin who had a garage in Caulfield.

"It is too far away," said the Fisherman, but the real reason was that Yoshi would charge him twice as much.

"Alright, you're killing me, but I will pay ten large, provided that you do the other thing," said Syd. The other thing was something that the Fisherman had been putting off for a long time.

"OK," he said quietly.

The Imperial was next door to Syd's office and not somewhere he liked to be seen. It was not kosher, and his wife would not like it either. In fact, Syd was very fond of a chicken parmigiana which they would deliver to the rear door so no one would see him in the pub. He told himself that chooks these days lived a good life and that modern butchery was put pretty much the same as kosher. He just did not tell his wife. If you met her you would understand, he was fond of saying.

"Okay, Eagle?" asked the Fisherman.

"Of course," replied Syd.

The fee would be deposited in an old Nescafé tin in the Fisherman's shed. The phrase that they had developed was "the Eagle in the nest" or "Eagle". Perhaps a little dramatic but Syd really liked 1960 spy movies and considered himself a modern Oscar Schindler, smuggling bodies or bags through occupied territories. For a fee, of course. He especially liked to speak in code.

"When?" asked the Fisherman.

"Wednesday, Baltic Princess, 5 am or thereabouts," said Syd the Squid quickly.

"Late pickup," said the Fisherman.

A 5 am pickup was all very well but the time to run up the Bay to drop the usual drop-off point would mean that it would be almost dawn when the Fisherman arrived back up the Bay. He preferred earlier pickups and a drop-off in the dark. However, it was dependent on the timing of the ships' run through the Heads. It was a risk, but he really needed the money, a matter which did not escape Syd the Squid.

"Can't be helped," said Syd the Squid.

"Delivery?" asked the Fisherman.

"Quarantine?" asked the Fisherman, being a reference to the usual pickup place namely Quarantine Bay, just inside Port Phillip heads.

"Yes," said Syd the Squid.

"Okay," said the Fisherman, although he was not all that happy.

Syd left his untouched tonic water and left the bar; the Fisherman finished his beer and another one too. He calculated the time it would take to run down the Bay to be inside the Heads at Quarantine Bay by 2 am. He always arrived early to ensure that he could watch the big boat come in through the Rip from the calm water of Quarantine Bay.

Wednesday came and the weather was less than optimal, a stiff southerly ruffling the water well up into the Bay. Molly and the Fisherman worked hard to beat down the Bay against wind and tide. Normally a dry boat, sheets of spray soon drenched the Fisherman. He dragged on his wet weather gear and felt better although his face and hands were soon without feeling.

Chapter 17

He had taken over the body and bag trade from his father who had dabbled in it during the post-war years. The Painters and Dockers had run it then although Yanni the mechanic was also involved in it from time to time. The Painters and Dockers had handed it over to Syd the Squid in return for some creative tax advice which kept the local union secretary out of jail, at least for a while. "Body" was exactly that, a crew member usually from one of the Baltic states who decided that he would like to emigrate to Australia, without the paperwork. Once safely inside the Heads a crewman would signal with a torch. The Fisherman would slip quietly into the boat's wake, invisible to its radar. Once he received the flash from the Fisherman's torch the crewman would jump over the stern. The crewman dressed in black was next to invisible but the chemical light stick, cracked in the crewman's hand, was all the Fisherman needed to find him.

The pilot boat usually followed the boat in it but on these nights would mysteriously decide to overtake the boat and run on the opposite side, away from the Fisherman's boat. The pilot boat driver would later quietly take a tightly rolled bundle of banknotes from Avi, Syd's cousin, in the bar of the Queenscliff Hotel. It was a good arrangement for all concerned, especially Syd the Squid.

The frozen, gasping crewman would be hauled unceremoniously over the side of the boat by the Fisherman. Immediately thereafter he would be crammed into the secret compartment under the floor at the front of the boat. The frozen bedraggled crewmember would later be pushed over the side in the shallow waters off a foreshore park in Mentone, to be greeted by Tashi, Syd's brother-in-law, an accountant from Sandringham. The Fisherman barely slowed the boat down to heave the body over the side before hauling the sail tight to speed almost silently into the night. He liked to be on the mooring and on shore before first light.

The "bag" part was much easier. It involved a packet which neither the sender nor the recipient wanted to be delivered by Australia Post, perhaps for a variety of reasons, but mostly centred around the Crimes Act. The Fisherman's rule was simple, never open the bag and he never had. He would collect it from the black water with a boat hook. Thereafter, it was immediately stuffed into the compartment under the floor. Later he would toss it over the side in the shallows at Mentone to be collected by Tashi, in his dark waders towing a car battery in an old inner tube powering a flounder light. Anyone watching would think Tashi was another hapless flounder fisherman trudging along the foreshore with a light and a spear, dragging a car battery in an old inner tube behind. Tashi quite liked flounder and would often spear quite a few while he waited. He was not as religious as Syd.

Chapter 18

A visit to the Warthog

The trip down the Bay had been uneventful, save for a nasty southerly which made the journey home very wet and cold. Nonetheless, he dropped off the bag just before dawn as agreed and watched while it was collected by Tashi, resplendent in yellow wet weather gear, towing the inner tube and looking like a genuine flounder fisherman as, indeed, he was.

He was at the mooring by 7 am and decided to visit the auto scrapyard to discuss the crankcase. The boat engine was barely running on the way home and he had used the sails for most of the trip. He drove past the shed and retrieved the Eagle from the nest. With a roll of notes in his pocket that would have choked a horse, he cruised to an industrial estate in a lesser part of Dandenong, if that were possible.

The scrapyard was in a cul-de-sac with several other dodgy looking businesses adjacent, a sheet-metal works, an electroplater, a recycle depot and a heavily fortified building with black windows and closed-circuit cameras – the local outlaw motorcycle gang clubhouse. Heavyset bikies with wraparound sunglasses watched him suspiciously as he drove past the clubhouse and into the scrapyard. The scrapyard looked like any other automotive wreckers, surrounded by high fences and populated by rusting car bodies, stacked at least three high, in seemingly unorganised confusion. As is standard for scrapyards, there were several extremely nasty dogs on chains who proceeded to announce his entrance in loud terms. The scrapyard also had two significant structures upon it. First, a huge hydraulic compactor which was used for transforming the car bodies into blocks of compacted metal suitable for shipping to the Indian smelters and for eliminating evidence which could be used against the bikies. Secondly, a rundown building with a sign which stated "Office" above the door. A second sign demanded that all visitors report to the office upon arrival. A third, much smaller sign, informed those who entered did so at their own risk. The Fisherman wondered why the third sign was necessary, so much was apparent to anyone with half a brain, he thought to himself. After a moment's thought, he decided that the clientele would benefit from such a warning, they probably did not have the requisite intellect to work it out for themselves.

He parked the Kingswood well away from the reach of the dogs on the chain and entered the office. The office was all you would expect from an office in a cul-de-sac in an industrial estate in Dandenong, owned and operated by a shifty scrapyard merchant. It was dirty, the reception desk was a packing crate on two trestles, a clipboard and a pencil were on the packing crate, as was a computer of museum much antiquity. The air was redolent with fly spray, stale pizza, motor oil and other less savoury, but uncertain, odours. A wall-mounted air conditioner, rattling noisily, completed the atmosphere.

Yanni's cousin, Mustapha, or Mick as he preferred to be known, was a stocky younger fellow with a fake suntan, dyed blonde hair and the whitest fake teeth that the Fisherman had ever seen. He was reasonably likeable and had a big smile with a gold tooth specially added to the dentures. He liked gold. He had many necklaces and even more bracelets made of thick bright yellow 24 carat gold. He was the opposite of Yanni, who was a taciturn difficult fellow with bad teeth and very little hair. Mick had a lot of hair, albeit dyed blonde, but a lot of undyed hair on his back, arms, legs, chest and abdomen. This prolific body hair also gave him his other name, "The Warthog". This was one of his two stage names, both of which he encouraged on every opportunity. He used the stage names when he was involved in his other career, making pornographic movies for family and friends, mainly the South Dandenong of the outlaw motorcycle gang "The Bastards". It was their clubhouse which was next door to the scrapyard.

He had adopted the stage name "The Warthog" because it reminded him of one of his porn industry heroes, "The Hedgehog", for whom he had enormous regard in a professional sense and also a significant collection of his works on DVD. In fact, he drew great inspiration from the collected works of "The Hedgehog" and copied the DVD plotlines assiduously in his own work. His other stage name was "Big Mick", another homage, this time to "Big John", a particular hero to Mick. "Big John" was so named because his downstairs equipment was of elephantine proportions. Mick was not in the same category, but with some careful editing no one could tell the difference. Mick was very good at digital editing.

Chapter 18

The movies were made upstairs in the office or in the bar of the motorcycle clubhouse. Each was different and, depending upon Mick's artistic sensibilities, were used to achieve different "moods", as he liked saying. In truth, the choice of location depended upon the weather, the upstairs room at the office got very warm in summer, whereas the bar was air-conditioned, albeit with an audience.

As for the cast, Mick had a steady supply of biker girlfriends, who would happily participate in return for screen credits and a large amount of Bolivian marching powder. They were, indeed, happy to engage in Mick's creative or more unusual plots, a matter that he found most useful, creative even, and which required several takes of each scene. The screen credits were happily provided by Mick, the marching powder by the bikies in return for a bulk deal on the DVDs and somewhat limited distribution rights.

It was a good relationship.

In order to sweeten the deal, Mick threw in the use of his industrial metal compactor. Untold numbers of bodies were in the boots of an untold numbers of cars, each of which were subsequently compacted and sent to India for smelting and to be reused as steel ingots.

Life was good.

Mick entered the room and upon seeing the Fisherman, raised his arms, embraced him and said "Maaaaaate". Mick was nothing if not likeable and colloquial. "Have you come about that part I offered you?" he said enthusiastically, whilst embracing the Fisherman in a bear hug.

"Not really," said the Fisherman.

"Why not, you would be perfect for it," said Mick, holding him tighter.

"Not really my scene," said the Fisherman, trying to push Mick away.

"Too bad, maybe next time," said Mick. "How about a box set of one of our special series, you know, I still have some left for special customers," added Mick.

"Haven't watched the last ones yet," said the Fisherman.

"Plenty of time, long cold nights on the boat, you know what I mean?" said Mick all that while embracing the Fisherman.

"Jasmine not working today?" asked the Fisherman noticing that Mick's wife was not behind the reception desk as usual. Mick paused and said, "She fucked off on me, took up with one of the extras from her last film." He added "bitch". After a short pause he continued, "We are still friends, and she has agreed to make a new series of DVDs for Christmas," he said brightly. "The boys next door are really looking forward to them," he added.

Jasmine, or Jasmine Juggs to use her stage name, was a popular performer in Mick's videos. Indeed, she had recently made several in which she starred including a "best of" compilation. Her videos were very popular especially after her recent anatomical enhancements.

"Sorry mate, didn't know," said the Fisherman who quite liked Jasmine, but not in a professional way. "Good to hear she has not retired, I am sure that her fans will be relieved," he added.

"More than you know." he said, with a big smile, showing his gold tooth.

"I need a new crankcase," said the Fisherman returning to the purpose of his visit.

"Yeah, Yanni told me," said Mick. "I've got exactly what you need," he added.

"1974, Datsun 120Y, that's what Yanni said," replied the Fisherman.

"Anything from '68 to '83 would be okay," said Mick.

"Okay, but I need it now," said the Fisherman.

"Don't get your net in a knot, I have plenty of them," said Mick, happily.

"Okay, well let's go and get one," replied the Fisherman.

Together they walked out of the office and into the scrapyard, Mick picking his way unerringly through three stories of car bodies in various states of decomposition. He paused at the base of the three-story sculpture comprising various Japanese rusting car bodies and said, pointing upwards, "that's the one". "Give me a minute and I will get it down for you," he added.

He reappeared with a very large forklift and proceeded to reorganise the car bodies like stacking a deck of cards. Within 30 minutes, the

Chapter 18

crankcase was on a forklift and gently deposited into the boot of the Fisherman's car.

"Thanks, how much?" asked the fisherman.

"$8,500" said Mick smiling broadly, showing his gold tooth.

"Yanni said the whole job would cost $5,000, including the crankcase," said the Fishermen tightly.

"Costs have gone up since then, and don't forget the Australian dollar has depreciated against the Yen," said Mick, brightly.

"You don't have any fucking costs, you bought this fucking land from the motorcycle gang for cash, and the fucking Yen has nothing to do with it," said the Fisherman. "Don't try and fuck me around," he added.

"Maaaaate, that was before the discount … For you…" He paused, obviously working out possibilities and continued "$850". He smiled broadly whilst doing so."Together with a boxed set of DVDs, 'The Classic Moments'," he added proudly.

"That would be great," said the Fisherman quickly, counting out the money as he did so.

He drove out of the scrapyard, reminding himself yet again, never to trust Mick or Yanni in matters involving money, life, or anything in between.

Slackwater

Chapter 19

Craypots, octopus and eels

All commercial fishermen in the top of the Bay would quietly catch crayfish. In his grandfather's day there was no licensing or quota system for crayfish, and you could catch as many as you were able. By the time his father was commercially fishing, crayfish were in big demand and the licences were too expensive. However, the Fisherman still set pots to catch them, it was just what you did, and he did not see the need for an expensive licence. He used small collapsible pots made from old reinforcing rods and chicken wire. They were kept under the floor of the boat and assembled out of sight of land. He would sell the catch quietly at the rear of the fish restaurant or to Jimmy at the Chinese restaurant in Graham Street. No questions were asked, and the money was good. Eric the fisheries inspector knew about this trade but turned a blind eye in exchange for a few at Christmas time. His wife Edna, a large woman with an unfortunate disposition, was very fond of crayfish especially at Christmas time.

The pots would also return with unwanted customers, mainly octopus and eels. The Fisherman hated octopus with a passion. They were unpleasant and difficult animals and he did not like the way they looked at him. Worst of all, it was not the bait that they were after but the crayfish. They would watch and wait until a crayfish was in the pot and then they would slide in after it and demolish it leaving only the shell. Octopus preferred eating crayfish above anything else. When the pot was hauled in it would change the colour of its skin from marbled brown to dark red, a sign of anger or aggression. The Fisherman would wrestle it from the craypot and kill it with a sharp bait knife. He would throw the lifeless now white body into a bucket to be used for bait. They were quite good bait, but it did not make up for the lost crayfish. He knew that the local Greek community liked to eat them, although he could not understand why one would need such disgusting looking things in preference to a nice piece of fish or better still a crayfish. There was probably a market to be had in fishing for them and selling them to those who would eat them, but he really did not care for it.

Eels were also caught in the craypots. He did not mind eels so much because they did not eat the crayfish, they were only interested in the bait. The problem with eels was that they were extremely difficult to grab and pull from the pot and very difficult to kill. They were strong and sinuous and covered with the slipperiest slime of any fish in the sea. There were two types of eels which he would get in the craypots. The first were his least favourite, conger eels. They were very large often as thick as his calf and were equipped with teeth like a dog. They were aggressive once caught in the craypot and would not let go of anything that they'd bite. He would open the top of the craypot to get access and entice them to bite the ebony donger or an old screwdriver. They would quickly oblige, and he would lift the struggling fish with the item that they were firmly fastened upon and with a single cut remove its head. The writhing bleeding body would thrash on the deck whilst the head still firmly bit down on the screwdriver or the old ebony ruler, glaring at him with deeply malevolent eyes. It would take some effort to prize the teeth from the screwdriver or ebony ruler. Each time he did so there were deep gouges in the metal or the ebony wood. However, they were very good eating, although difficult to sell to the modern consumer. Those who understood conger eel would happily buy them. Jimmy at the Chinese restaurant was very fond of them, although the fish restaurant would not buy them. This was not because they did not like them, but because they knew they could not be sold as conger eel as no one would buy them. Occasionally, the proprietor of the fish restaurant would buy them cheaply and sell them as a more marketable fish fillet and no one would know the difference. Such was the sleight of hand which was common in the retail marketing of seafood products. It did not trouble the Fisherman.

The second type of eel were short finned eels which he would also catch in the river. These eels, although they lived most of their life in fresh or brackish water, would travel into the saltwater and out to sea to spawn. It was then that they would come into the craypots. These were very good eating and whilst as slippery as a conger eel they were not as nasty. The Fisherman liked them and at one time there was a good market for them, although not for some time. The Vietnamese restaurant in Port Melbourne, which had opened in the mid-1970s, was his only market these days. He would often keep them himself

Chapter 19

and grill them on the old wooden barbecue in the backyard. He would invite Oleg to come and eat eels with him. Oleg was very partial to eels, it must be a Russian thing, the Fisherman thought. Oleg would bring vodka and they would spend a pleasant evening eating grilled eels and drinking vodka. Oleg didn't talk much which suited the Fisherman very well.

Chapter 20

The Fisherman is thrown from the boat

It was the coldest day for 25 years, make no mistake about that. The tender was covered in frost when he arrived in the morning fog. His hands hurt when he touched the oars as he rowed to the boat. He did his best to ignore the bitter cold because he needed to go out that morning. Once again, the bills were piling up and he knew that he could only ignore them for so long. Winter was a hard time for the Fisherman. The mornings were cold and the fishing was hard. The cold made his hands hurt and his back and knees ached abominably. That is not so say that winter fishing was bad, it was just very hard. Indeed, winter fishing could be surprisingly good. On still mornings, he would often find good schools of garfish near the old pier and snapper in the reefs near the channel marker. Sometimes he would find mullet schooling near the river mouth but only after the full moon.

He was hopeful of a few boxes of fish which he may be able to sell to the restaurants, if only the Indian restaurant for curry. Garfish, on the other hand, would be a premium fish which he could sell to the fish restaurant on the old railway line. A big snapper would be a bonus. It was with that in mind, and also the impending payment dates of the bills, that he sculled the tender into the dark before dawn.

As usual he was fishing on his own. He had been fishing on his own since he was young and certainly since the demise of his grandfather and then his father. He did not mind fishing on his own in the boat, indeed in some ways he preferred it. But there was something to be said for some company on the long days especially when the fishing was slow, as it often was these days.

He was familiar with handling the boat on his own and could manage the tasks that were required. He would haul the sail, set the net, and retrieve the net even when it was well laden with fish.

He coaxed the old diesel into life, tied the tender on to the mooring and cast off. The diesel rattling noisily in the dark, coughing occasionally with the cold. As usual on a cold morning he steered with the tiller between his legs standing up in the stern of the boat, his hands deep in his pockets, moving from side to side trying to keep warm. When the sun came up, he would normally tie off the tiller and make his way round the boat, baiting hooks, readying the net and ensuring that everything was where it needed to be. However, it was so cold that he could not bring himself to do the normal tasks. Shortly before dawn the southerly breeze picked up and a short nasty chop was quartering on the bow and then shifted amidships. A light drizzling rain came over the boat in the squall. The deck was slippery with some diesel he had spilled earlier. He was not quite dosing, but neither was he as alert as he should have been when a larger than normal wave hit the boat square amidships. The boat ran down the wave awkwardly. Before he could react, the boat lurched violently, and was suddenly into the trough. He was thrown overboard.

He entered the water backwards, his hands still deep in the pockets of his woollen jacket. The water was so cold it burned like fire. The shock of the coldness snatched the breath from his lungs. For a few seconds he was immobile, paralysed by cold, incredulous that he had allowed this to happen after all his experience and time on the water. This was the moment that his father and grandfather had warned him about. This was the moment that they had said they were so deeply afraid of. To be thrown from the boat, alone in the water, with no one to know where you were, and no one to know where you died. His old heavy woollen jacket was dragging him down, his sea boots and thick woollen socks heavy. Both were intent on killing him. He tried to shrug off the jacket, but it clung to him like a shroud. He kicked off one gumboot and focused on unburdening himself from the jacket. Precious seconds passed by. He sank deeper. He freed one arm from the jacket and then another, his lungs on fire. He sank deeper. Finally, he was relieved of the other gumboot and kicked to the surface. The only thing on his mind was that he would not allow himself to die in the way that his grandfather had warned him of.

After an eternity, he broke the surface and gasped for air. He was rewarded with a mixture of air and saltwater in equal measure. The saltwater burned his lungs and he coughed violently only to swallow more saltwater. Coughing and dry retching, he tread water with legs that were rapidly becoming dysfunctional in the cold. The boat was circling about 200 metres away pitching violently in the nasty chop. He could feel the strength ebbing from his arms and legs, draining away rapidly in the cold. He knew that unless he did something, he would certainly die. His eyes burning with salt he saw a channel marker which

Chapter 20

was closer than the boat. He did not think he could swim as far as the boat but hoped that he could swim as far as the channel marker.

Unlike most fishermen, including his grandfather and father, he was a competent swimmer, they on the other hand could not swim. His grandfather, like many men of his time, had never been taught to swim and considered it to be a professional weakness. In his grandfather's view, you did not need to know how to swim unless you intended to capsize the boat or otherwise behave in a fashion unbecoming of a seaman. Nonetheless, his grandfather always had a nagging fear that he would one day be claimed by the sea. His father, on the other hand, had a more prosaic view. The school which his father had attended in Port Melbourne did not have a swimming pool and he had not been taught how to swim. Nonetheless, like most children living by the sea, he had learned how to swim in a fashion after jumping from the pier with his friends on hot days. He knew that as a weak swimmer he was at risk in the boat, but circumstances were such that it was the only living that he knew, and he depended upon it for his livelihood.

He struck out for the channel marker swimming awkwardly in the heavy chop, desperately trying to reach it before his strength gave out. He tried to time his breaths between the chop so he would not take in mouthfuls of burning saltwater. It was virtually impossible not to, so he tried to breathe as little as possible. This was not helpful either as his strength was rapidly draining away from exposure and acidosis. He made the channel marker, the large floating metal buoy, anchored to the seafloor and with a metal superstructure adorned with a flashing red light. The channel marker was pitching violently from side to side in the heavy chop and also heaving vertically. Treading water adjacent to it he was wary of coming too close lest his skull was crushed by the thick steel. He waited until there was a gap between the chop and launched himself at the channel marker. It was mistimed, and the metal superstructure cracked him on the elbow as it heaved in his direction. It missed his skull by a few centimetres for which he was relieved, but his arm was barely functional. He knew that he only had seconds remaining before he would be unable to tread water any longer and would drown within sight of the channel marker. Kicking with both legs and his good arm he grabbed the marker and got a good grip on the superstructure. He hooked his bad arm through the elbow around the superstructure and was able to crawl up on the rocking buoy. His weight steadied the channel marker somewhat and although his situation was precarious, he felt most relieved to be out of the water.

By this time the sun was over the horizon, the fog had lifted, and he could see the boat noisily circling several hundred metres away. The wind had died down and the sea became calmer. He was warmer out of the water but soon was shivering uncontrollably. The winter sun did little to warm him, but it was a comfort, nonetheless. After half an hour or so, he stopped shivering and began to feel warm. He learned later that this was his body shutting down and that he was dying. Semiconscious he heard a voice and a noisy outboard motor. He looked up to see Carlo, the old Italian bloke, who was often fishing for squid in the dawn near the channel marker. Carlo was a retired solicitor who, after his most recent divorce had relocated from Brighton leaving the most recent Mrs Carlo with a very nice renovated Victorian house in Brighton. Carlo was currently sharing a flat in Port Melbourne with Agnes, his former secretary. The Fisherman did not hold any of that against Carlo, certainly not in the present circumstances. Carlo had set out just after dawn, intent on a feed of calamari. He had seen the Fisherman's boat circling and motored over to it in his old tinnie. He knew that something was wrong, but he was relieved to see the Fisherman hanging onto the channel marker.

"You look like shit," said Carlo, as he hauled the Fisherman into his boat. The Fisherman tried to speak but he could not, his jaw was frozen from the cold. He lay in the bottom of the tinnie barely conscious.

The Fisherman did not know what happened next, but he did remember being dragged across the sand by the elderly Italian man and into his car. After half an hour of the heater in the car going full speed the Fisherman felt a little better. He mumbled a thank you. It was not clear if Carlo heard, but if he did, he did not acknowledge it. They both knew that the Fisherman would have died before long and they were both somewhat embarrassed, each in different ways. The Fisherman because it happened, Carlo because it was his way. Such is the way of old-fashioned men.

Thereafter, he would deliver Carlo a fat snapper or some shiny mullet on a regular basis. They never spoke of that day, and never would. Each knew that it was significant, each knew that they had no words.

Chapter 21

Local politics

The local member for the ALP was Bob Liversidge, Liver Damage to his friends, of which he had few real ones. In the 35 years in which he had been a member of the Lower House he had not made a speech in Parliament, let alone a maiden speech, and spent most days in the front bar of the Sandridge or the Imperial, both of which he quite liked. He was known as Liver Damage for reasons which were apparent upon meeting him. Red-faced, vague and speedy to agree with whatever was your point of view. If asked, he would say, meaningfully, "I will take it straight to the Premier". This usually got him another drink, which was his sole purpose in life. The problem was that the ALP was under siege from the Greens. Liver Damage could not cut it with the sharp, university educated Greens. They had an answer for everything, they looked so fresh and shiny. Liver Damage looked old, shabby and drunk, which, of course, he was.

The old guard from Port Melbourne knew Liver Damage, he was one of them, he knew and understood them. In fact, he had been to school with most of them. They trusted him to the extent that they could, which was not much, but everyone liked him. They also knew if he was offered a job as the Chairperson of the Sludge Abatement Board that he would drop them in a heartbeat. There was comfort, however, in his predictability. Also, they knew that he would never scale the lofty heights of the Sludge Abatement Board. He was theirs forever, unless he was fucked over by the Evil Greens; as time went on, a more realistic possibility.

The problem was the influx of nasty, evil, Green voters. They wanted to turn the Port into a worker's (university educated) paradise. They wanted it to be a GM free, nuke free, organic, pesticide free, rainbow, refugee friendly, politically correct paradise. Sadly, the demographic was lapping it up. 150 years of history were about to be flushed away.

The fishing got a lot better after the scallop boats were banned from the Bay. It took a few years but slowly the snapper ran back to their familiar spawning grounds and life was good. Just when he thought things had turned around, the State Government urged on by some "greenie garden fairies", as he described them, decided to buy back the commercial fishing licences.

"The Bay is for recreational fishing," said the Premier smiling broadly, flanked by nodding heads. "It is not a place for commercial fishing, everyone has a right to catch a fish on the weekend," said the Premier, a former union shop steward with a nasty temper who hated fishing but liked being the Premier.

"Bastards," said Bill the Younger, watching the television news in the bar.

"Fuckers," said Errol.

"This will do more harm than good," said the Fisherman. "Every prick with a fishing rod will catch anything that moves. No one will throw anything back. It will kill the Bay," he predicted.

"What are you gonna do?" asked Errol. "The buyback sounds good," he added. "They might get away with it."

The truth of it was the years had been bad for as long as he could remember, and the thought of a nice payout seemed pretty good. He telephoned the Department, as he had been told to do. He was told "Lodge an expression of interest", the website also said this, whatever the fuck that meant. There was a form to fill in. He filled in the form, overstating his income from fishing for the last five years by about ten times. Phil helped him with that part. Phil knew a lot about how to fill in a form and make things a lot better than they were. "That should do it," said Phil. On Phil's advice he ignored the part that said he needed to attach tax returns for the last five years. Phil was sure they wouldn't notice, and, in any event, he didn't have any.

He posted the form by giving it to Marjorie in the post office. Marjorie was Bill's cousin and had always been keen on the Fisherman. He made small talk with Marjorie and got out of the post office as fast as he could, having promised Marjorie that he would call in again soon. "You dodged a bullet there," Bill would say, "Marjorie would talk you to death and then start again". Marjorie also came from a long line of wowsers, meaning parsimonious women, from Bill's late mother's side of the family. Bill was always keen to point that distinction out, albeit in private.

Chapter 21

The response from the Department was slow but finally arrived. The letter pointed out that he must provide documentary proof of his income before the expression of interest could proceed further. However, it went on to outline the "proper measure" of compensation. Apparently, the government did not have to pay him a penny and was offering, or might offer, money out of the goodness of the government's heart. This was despite the Premier's effusive and generous predictions that no fisherman would be worse off.

The letter continued by outlining a scheme which it described as being based upon a five-year assessment of profit, extrapolated to a lifetime average with a discount for net present value.

"What the fuck is that?" he asked Phil.

Phil, who had a lifetime of dealing with government departments said, "It means that they will pay fuck all, but only if you can prove it."

"Fuckers," said Errol.

"Ffffucking oath," said Phil.

"Shit," said the Fisherman.

"You need to speak to Bob," said Bill the Younger.

Bob, as everyone knew, was as shrewd as they come, having been a life insurance salesman for 15 years before entering Parliament. He was fond of saying that he entered Parliament, "So I could make a difference". In truth, he lost his job in insurance and had stood for Parliament because he thought the money would be better than he had been paid and it was a job for eight years. He couldn't believe it when he was elected. His longevity was due to the fact that no one in Port Melbourne wanted anything from the government. Most of them were engaged in some type of welfare scam and did not want to draw attention to themselves. This meant that Bob could support anything that he liked and, with a little forward planning, he was returned each time at the ballot box. Life was good and meant that most afternoons when Parliament was sitting and every day when it was not, Bob was in attendance at the Imperial. Bob had also developed a sixth sense which told him whenever a constituent entered the bar and wanted something from him. He would dart into the dunny and listen to the small radio which he stashed behind the cistern in the cubicle. The citizen would eventually get bored and leave, Bob re-emerging after the publican,

Bob's brother-in-law, banged on the wall behind the bar. It was a good arrangement and suited Bob well. However, the system fell down when the Fisherman quietly walked into the room. Bob looked up to see the Fisherman heading straight for him.

"Call of nature," he said. "Might take some time, a dodgy prawn curry from the Raj." He disappeared into the men's room like a rat up a drainpipe. Unperturbed, the Fisherman, who well knew Bob's method of operation, followed him into the toilet. Outside the cubicle he explained to Bob that the Department needed to stick their net present value up their arses and pay him, say, $200,000.

"Can't a man have some peace?" whined Bob from behind the door.

"Mate, I've voted for you for decades," the Fisherman lied. "And never asked for anything". The latter was mostly true if a reduction in the amount of the council rates on his house were excluded not that Bob did anything about that anyway.

"It's a matter for the Department," said Bob. "Anyway, the Premier is hot to trot on this stuff and nothing is going to change."

"The Premier is a turd who thinks this will get him re-elected," said the Fisherman. "All I want is a fair thing," he added.

"I can't do anything about it," pleaded Bob.

"I guess if Sharni wanted some help you'd offer to help her," said the Fishermen. He knew nothing about Sharni but Bill the Younger had told him that Bob had a fixation with the young Indian waitress at the Raj named Sharni. He would get takeaway from the Raj regularly even though Mrs Liversidge did not like Indian particularly, she preferred a nice spaghetti bolognese. Bob didn't much like Indian food either, especially from the Raj, but he did quite like Sharni.

There was a silence behind the cubicle door. Bob was thinking fast, although this phenomenon was quite relative in terms of its speed.

"I guess I could write a letter," he said hopefully.

"To the Premier," said the Fisherman.

"Of course," said Bob, with as much conviction as he could muster, sitting on a cracked pedestal in the smoke-stained lavatory cubicle.

"Thanks Bob," said the Fisherman.

Chapter 21

A few days later Bob materialised in the Sandridge. He gave the Fisherman a copy of the letter which he had typed but not sent to the Premier. It went into great detail about the importance of the local economy of commercial fishing and the need to do the right thing as far as compensation was concerned. It was not a bad letter and may have had some effect, but Bob had not sent it, he had been one of the Premier's key supporters in the buyback, unbeknown to the good residents of his electorate.

"The Premier called me immediately after I sent this," Bob lied well after all his years of practice. "He will take it up with the Department personally," he continued.

"What next?" asked the Fisherman.

"Things move slowly in government, old boy," said Bob reassuringly, feeling pretty good by now.

Months later, and despite calls to the Department, who kept stonewalling about tax returns, and who appeared not to know about the Premier's personal intervention, the Fisherman gave up. He kept fishing and sold locally, no one seemed to notice. He removed the licence numbers from the bow of his boat. No one bothered him and he was happy.

"What happened about the buyback?" asked Bill.

"Nothing," said the Fisherman.

"Bob said that he had fixed it," said Bill the Younger.

"Bullshit," said the Fisherman.

"Fucker," said Errol.

"Fffffucking oath," said Phil.

"Arsehole," said Bill.

Slackwater

Chapter 22

The hardware shop

After his delightful dealing with Muhammad regarding the fish, the Fisherman went to pick up some items at the hardware shop around the corner from the pub. The hardware shop had been in business for as long as anyone could remember, that is after it had been a milk bar. The milk bar had been owned by Nick, an old Italian. It had a bell over the door which rang when you entered the odd smelling shop. The smell was hard to articulate but probably a rustic blend of mildew, cigarette smoke, rotten onions and potatoes from the small shelf near the door.

Nick would appear from the back room where he lived and served the odd customer. He was taciturn and silent, offering out of date tinned food, cigarettes and newspapers with equal enthusiasm. The milk was fresh provided it was a Monday, if not, it was better left on the shelf. There were two local Nicks and it was important to identify each one so as not to cause confusion. "Which Nick?" would be the inquiry. "Italian Nick or Greek Nick?" would be added. Greek Nick ran the fish and chip shop which sold good fish and chips (frozen fish only) and quite acceptable burgers (although he never could understand beetroot). Greek Nicks was a decent place to eat or buy takeaway.

Italian Nicks was a milk bar and only good to buy newspaper or cigarettes. Accordingly, it was important to clarify which Nick was being discussed.

At all events, the milk bar was sold by Rosa, Italian Nick's widow after he died of a heart attack. The heart attack was probably brought about by the sudden engagement announcement of Mary, Nick's daughter to an insurance salesman from Williamstown. This, together with the announcement of pregnancy a few days later, was all too much for Italian Nick, a staunch Catholic and lifelong hater of insurance companies.

The shop was purchased by Harry who knew nothing about milk bars but had worked in a hardware shop on and off for most of his life. This on and off work experience was largely due to several periods of incarceration mainly for dealing in stolen goods. Harry's great love was not in hardware but as a fence, that is to say, a handler of stolen goods or at least those of dubious provenance. He liked nothing better than buying jewellery and other items from local villains and to resell them for a profit. These transactions were exclusively undertaken in the bars of the local pubs, where Harry could engage in his other great love, beer.

Unfortunately for Harry, he was not very good at being a fence mainly because it did require some discretion. Further, everyone including Murray, the local police officer, knew that Harry was a fence who drank too much. Harry often drank at the Sandridge but never "worked" at the Sandridge having promised Young Bill that he would not engage in his chosen profession within the walls of the Sandridge.

This did not stop Murray calling in to chat with Harry at the Sandridge but so far had never resulted in an arrest at the Sandridge. A matter which was pleasing to Bill, but in truth reflected Murray's respect for Bill's father. Harry sold a small range of hardware from the shop. It was not a franchise hardware store so he could stock what he liked. The shop sold the usual suspects, nails, screws, hammers and a few power tools. There were also a large range of herbicides and pesticides to cater for the local community's preference for weed free concrete backyards and fly free barbeques. Harry, who lived at the rear of the shop, would open on a Sunday for locals if you pressed the concealed buzzer near the top of the door. You need to understand that this was in the days when Sunday trading was illegal. Whilst this was remnant of illegal Sunday trading, it suited Harry who did not like attending the shop on weekends. He preferred watching the greyhounds or the trots on the cable television.

Harry also sold a variety of fishing equipment and maritime chandlery which was why the Fisherman was a regular customer for new fishing line, hooks and other bits and pieces. In a shed at the rear of the property, Harry also had a small compressor and equipment for filling scuba tanks. Harry knew nothing about scuba diving and did not care for it all, being unable to swim. He had purchased the compressor from the proprietor of a small scuba diving shop in Graham Street which had gone broke. The proprietor had equated the proximity to the sea with a desire of the locals to explore scuba diving. Nothing could have been further from the truth, indeed, most of the locals could not swim. Harry did know how to make money, and he soon realised that if the tanks were filled quickly in a half full bath of water they would fill with hot air.

Chapter 22

When filled quickly in the water bath the gauge would register full, but once the air cooled inside the tank, it would read much less maybe half. However, the customer would not know until several hours later when the tank had cooled down. The result was a half full tank for a full tank price.

Harry also economised on the filters for the compressor, which were quite expensive. He would wash the old ones and dry them on the concrete in the back yard rather than fitting new ones. The result was half a tank full of oily air which would not kill you but would give you a blinding headache.

Hot Fill Harry, as he was known, was the refiller of last resort for the local scuba divers. On the positive side, Harry was obliging and would open up the shop and fill tanks whenever the concealed button was pressed.

The Fisherman walked into the shop, the bell above the door announcing his entry. Harry was behind the counter, attaching price tags with little bits of string to some cheap Chinese multigrips, which he had bought from Bunnings earlier that day.

"How about some new pliers?" he said. "Got them on special."

"No more of that cheap Chinese shit," said the Fisherman. "The last one rusted up before I had a chance to use it."

"There is no guarantee against rust or saltwater damage," said Harry quickly. "Anyway, you have to look after tools," he added, knowing that they would rust in the refrigerator, such was their poor quality.

"Got any 25-pound mono in 500-yard spools?" the Fisherman asked.

"It doesn't come like that anymore," said Hot Fill. "You can get 12 kg in 250 metre spools. It is about the same."

"That will do, but none of that braid shit," said the Fisherman. "Don't like it and it is too expensive."

"Everyone uses braid," said Hot Fill.

"Not me," retorted the Fisherman.

"I have some out the back," said Harry disappearing into a dark doorway. Harry reappeared with the fishing line and a shiny stainless steel turnbuckle in the other hand.

"I got the turnbuckle you wanted too," he said happily.

"Right," said the Fisherman. "Can I put them on the slate?" presuming the cost of the turnbuckle would be greater than the available funds in his wallet. Seeing the pained expression on Hot Fill's face he added, "I'll settle up next week."

"I guess so," said Harry glumly, dropping both into a paper bag. The Fisherman took the bag and went to leave as quickly as he could, in case Harry changed his mind.

"Haven't seen Murray about for a few days, have you?", inquired Hot Fill, his eyes glancing away nervously.

"Nope, maybe he is visiting his daughter in Warrnambool," replied the Fisherman. "Are you working Harry?" he asked.

"No," Harry said quickly, "But I am meeting a bloke at the Imperial later, don't want to be harassed by that bastard."

"Whatever you say Harry," he said over his shoulder as he opened the door, the bell clanging loudly.

Chapter 23

Back at the pub

He cruised from the hardware shop around the corner to the pub. It was about lunchtime he figured. As usual the occupants of the bar turned to look as he entered the room. A few greetings of "mate", or "g'day" were uttered before they returned to their beers or form guides or both. Oleg glanced over the top of his form guide to check that he was not a suit. He said nothing. Young Bill, resplendent in a red hula shirt and blond toupee (one of his favourites), poured a beer and set it in front of the Fisherman's stool.

"How did you go with the fish?" he enquired.

"Muhammad," the Fisherman replied.

"Better than nothing," said Young Bill.

"Not much fucking better," said the Fisherman.

"That little prick is like a rat with a gold tooth, always pleased with himself when he is dudding someone else," said Bill.

"Fucker," said Errol.

"F-f-f-fucken oath," said Phil.

"Another one, Fabulous?" said Young Bill pouring a beer.

"Wwwhy nnnot," stammered Phil. The frosty glass appeared in front of him within a few seconds.

"Pie?" asked Bill looking at the Fisherman whilst pointing at the pie warmer behind the bar. The pie warmer and the frozen pies had been a deal that Bill had done with Hot Fill. A matter of an outstanding bar tab which needed to be settled. Everyone in the bar knew that the pies were way out of date and had been in the warmer for weeks.

"Maybe not today," he said. "How about a toasted sanga?"

"No worries," said Young Bill. There was only one type of toasted sandwich on the menu, cheese, onion and vegemite. In fact, that was the only thing on the menu, despite the stained menus in a pile on the bar.

There was not much call for meals these days and Young Bill had suggested to Theresa, the large Italian woman who cooked for the pub, that maybe she only needed to come in on Saturday nights. The arrangement suited Theresa who was rather tired of cooking chops and sausages with the occasional chicken parma. However, soon she decided that it was not worth her while to warm up a few pies on a Saturday.

The Fisherman was content with a toasted sandwich and knew that it was unlikely to be as bad as a pie.

While it was cooking, Young Bill poured new beers for those in need including the Fisherman.

Young Bill took the toasted sandwich out of the dirty toaster, cut it in half and placed it in front of the Fisherman. "Wrap your laughing gear around that," he said.

"Thanks," said the Fisherman, already gobbling it. He was hungrier than he thought which was just as well as you needed to be hungry to eat one of Bill's sandwiches. "How is the watch?" he asked, seeing Bill tapping the watch and holding it to his ear.

"Fucking thing keeps stopping," he said.

"H-h-h-hot Fill?" asked Phil.

"Yeah," said Bill. "Genuine Rolex he told me."

"Fucker," said Errol.

"F-f-f-fuckenoath," said Phil.

"Arsehole," said Oleg in his best Arnold Schwarzenegger imitation, which was not bad at all.

"Yeah," said Bill the Younger.

"A-a-a-ask for a r-r-refund," said Phil.

"I'll sort him out, don't you worry about that," said Bill.

"He's at the Imperial this arvo doing a bit of business," offered the Fisherman.

"Next time he comes in I'll have a word to him in his shell-like," said Bill.

"Fucking Norwegian," said Oleg from behind the form guide.

At about then the door into the bar creaked and a swarthy fellow in grubby overalls entered the room. Bob the Builder was a local builder of dubious ability. He was currently avoiding service of proceedings from the building ombudsman and had taken to passing himself off as "Yan", an Afghanistani concreter. He was much better at concreting

Chapter 23

than building and was making a quiet and good living constructing concrete floors, patios and carports, cash only of course.

"G'day Bob," said Bill the Younger.

"Yan," said Bob.

"Fucker," said Errol.

"Ffffuckenoath," said Phil.

Oleg briefly glanced over the top of his form guide. He figured that it was none of his business if a man gave himself a new identity.

"How's business?" asked Bill, sliding a beer in front of Bob.

"Not bad," said Bob. "Some fucking yuppie tried to pay me with a cheque the other day, wanted to know who to make it out to."

"Fucker," said Errol, staring into his beer.

"Yeah," said Phil, looking up from the crossword.

"Not very friendly of him," said Bill, remembering the last time he had seen someone try and pay Bob by cheque. It was as if Bob had been handed a live snake.

"Told him to stick it up his arse, only do cash jobs," said Bob.

"Ffffuckenoath,' said Phil.

"Pie?' asked Young Bill hopefully.

"Nah mate, toasted sanga," replied Bob quickly, who knew about the frozen pies.

Young Bill busied himself making a sandwich and placing it inside the antique toaster.

"Got a new job," said Bob after a slug of beer. "Big one for Syd the Squid."

"Syd the Squid?" asked the Fisherman incredulously.

"Jesus," said Young Bill; "Make sure you do a good job and count the money."

"I went to school with him," said Bob somewhat defensively.

"Then count it twice," said the Fisherman.

"Fucker," said Errol.

"Ffffuckenoath," stammered Phil, wide-eyed. Phil had dealings with Syd in the matter of a hire purchase plan, the so-called 'floor plan' for car dealerships. Unfortunately, the usual car financiers declined Phil's business after a series of consumer affairs prosecutions. Sydney Goldblatt offered to assist. It was the worst mistake Phil made, something that he would quickly admit although not to Syd the Squid.

"Irek and the fire had been a gift from God in so many ways," he would often say.

Chapter 24

Mending the nets and a visit from Spud

After lunch and a few beers, he eased into the Kingswood and cruised back to the house. It was still early, so he decided to make some repairs to the net hanging from the side fence the length of the driveway. He had snagged it on a reef a few weeks earlier and it was badly in need of repair. He made a cup of tea, found a biscuit in the old biscuit tin and went out to the shed. Here he found a thick needle and twine to weave a new panel in the net. Sitting on a stool in the afternoon sun he was quite happy weaving the new diamond pattern section. He became lost in concentration as the rhythmic weaving of the needle continued. A skill he had learned by watching his grandfather and father, it never failed to remind him of his childhood. He trimmed the ends with a small bait knife which he had honed on a whetstone so that it was razor-sharp. The little knife cut through the tough nylon like butter. He stood back and assessed the work, not without a little pride in a job well done.

A shortish, obese man walked heavily down the driveway, his face a pasty white, tinged with pink at the cheeks and around his small eyes.

"G'day," said the man.

"Spud," said the Fisherman.

Spud was so-called because of his general physique and facial appearance, just like a spud everyone agreed. Spud glared at him; he disliked the epithet, but it was too late because everyone called him Spud. He said it was because he worked in a local fruit and vegetable shop. In truth, it had nothing to do with that, everyone just thought he looked like a potato. His brother was of similar dimensions and physiognomy but with a decidedly pointy head. Accordingly, he was known as Spike. Spike did not care about being called Spike, in fact, he thought it was cool. Spike was not too bright, but he had a friendlier disposition than Spud.

"Got any bait?" asked Spud. The Fisherman would keep fish heads and frames for crayfish bait. He also had squid which he had caught but had not been able to sell. Frozen squid made good bait for fishing which he would often sell if asked. He also had frozen Australian salmon which he had not been able to sell as fresh fish.

"Squid or salmon?" he replied.

"Some of each," said Spud.

Spud followed him into the shed and waited while the Fisherman dove deep into the massive chest freezer in the shop.

"How many bodies can you fit in there?" asked Spud.

"Depends how fat they are," replied the Fisherman.

Spud glared darkly at him and thrust a crumpled $10 note into his hand. In return he took several kilos each of squid and salmon. A good deal. As he watched Spud waddle down the driveway he decided to go back to the net and remembered how much he disliked him. It needed new lead weights at the bottom to keep it taut in the water.

He found the sinker moulds in a wooden box in the shed. They were old cast aluminium moulds in pieces with a small hole in the side. Held together by a piece of wire, molten lead was poured in through a steel funnel to fill the moulds. Dropped into a bucket of cold water the sinkers could be turned out quite quickly. He busied himself setting out the moulds and melting some lead sheets in an old saucepan over a gas burner. He carefully placed the steel rod through the centre of the mould so that the sinkers would have a hole in the centre. A length of nylon would later pass through the centre of each, securing to the net.

The afternoon passed quickly as he made sufficient sinkers to replace those missing from the net. Afterwards he packed up the tools, moulds and the burner. He folded the net as best he could and stored it in the shed. It would be used when the time came to repair the net currently in the boat. He remembered the spool of new fishing line and retrieved it from the car, nodding to the old Greek woman in black stockings walking past with her small shopping trolley as he went. Rosa lived a few doors away; her husband Jim had died in an accident on the dock. She accepted fish from him from time to time. In return, he would find a bag of lemons or some parsley carefully wrapped in damp kitchen paper, hanging from his front door.

He tied one end of the monofilament to the clothes hoist in the centre of the backyard. Then he stretched tight from there around a tree and back until it was all stretched tightly. He would leave it overnight as his grandfather and father had shown him. It got rid of the coils they would say. He was not sure that modern monofilament needed it, but he did it, nonetheless. He never used braid unlike the new breed of commercial fishermen. Anyway, it was far too expensive.

He thought about sharpening some hooks and making some new ganged hooks for kingfish. He decided to leave those jobs until tomorrow, as it was getting dark. His eyesight was not what it used to be and opening the eye of the hook and threading through another required careful attention in good light.

He had no food for dinner and like most fishermen did not care for fish. He drove two blocks to the butcher shop run by Ken the Butcher. Ken was an old-style butcher with an old-style butcher shop. It had a big wooden block behind the counter and cleavers and steels hung on hooks. A rail system for moving carcasses hung from the ceiling before snaking into the cool room at the rear of the shop. Ken was red-faced and stocky, resplendent in a white T-shirt and blue striped apron. A chain belt around his ample waste supported a scabbard with several knives and a steel. Ken raised rabbits in his backyard for the shop together with some chooks for eggs and meat. He raced pigeons on the weekend from coops at the rear of the shop. Every Saturday night he went to the greyhound races, wearing a shiny suit a few sizes too small and a porkpie hat, also a few sizes too small.

A former Painter and Docker, he would often reminisce on life as a stevedore.

"Never paid for anything," he would say. "Fridges, stoves, the odd car, all were damaged on the manifest or disappeared overboard. The black bans we slapped on the boats worked like magic. The boat owners would do anything to get the boats unloaded back out on the sea."
"Mind you," he would say, "There was a code, the most senior bloke had the first pick of all the goods. Others followed in turn. But we all did okay."

Butchery came quite naturally to Ken; his father having been one all his life. When Ken Senior retired it seemed quite natural for him to take over. Ken Senior was a staunch unionist, like his father before him. More than once Ken Senior had been called in to assist with 'cleanup'. A cleanup involved disposing of the body, usually that of a rival unionist. Ken Senior was a magician, they said, he could dismember a body in under 30 minutes without breaking a sweat. On one occasion, Ken Senior sold the products of his labour to the cray fishermen as bait. It was pork they said, an export order of wild boar which was condemned due to salmonella contamination. They said it was fantastic bait and all came back for more.

"All gone," said Ken Senior.

"Pity," they all said.

Naturally Ken the Butcher was expected to follow in Ken Senior's footsteps which was of course what he did. Albeit too enthusiastically for some. Ken liked to be part of the business before the clean-up also. In time, Ken the Butcher gained something of a reputation as a standover man or enforcer. It was only natural that he would do 'odd jobs' for Syd the Squid. Locals treated Ken with respect and bought his meat which was always good. Most were circumspect about his sausages and preferred the supermarket ones. Not so the Fisherman. He thought Ken's sausages were outstanding. They had a certain quality and texture which the supermarket variety just could not match.

He pushed open the fly screen door just as Ken was cleaning up before closing.

"Just in time," said Ken.

"Sausages?" he asked.

"Yeah," said the Fisherman. "Any of those plain pork ones?"

"Plenty, back in a tick" said Ken. Ken disappeared into the cool room and emerged with a string of fat pork sausages. He wrapped them in white paper and handed them to the Fisherman. "Never met a sausage that I did not like," said Ken as he handed the parcel to the Fisherman.

He reached for his wallet only to be stopped by Ken.

"Don't worry, swap you for a few mullet."

"Okay," said the Fisherman. "There are plenty around at the moment".

"No worries," said Ken. "See you round like a rissole," he added.

"Butcher's joke," they both said in chorus. The Fisherman had heard the joke many times before.

He said goodbye and drove home slowly. After grilling the sausages under the old gas grill, he ate quickly, and had two fingers of Scotch. He went to bed. He was asleep within minutes with the alarm set for 4 am, as usual.

Chapter 25

A trip up the river and the last eel fisher

The next morning was still and clear with a nice crescent moon. He left the tender bobbing at the mooring and set off, the diesel coughing for a time before settling into an even rhythm. Fishing on the top of the Bay had gone quiet so he decided to run across to the mouth of the Maribyrnong River where it entered the Bay at Yarraville. In the old days, the Maribyrnong was a good source of eels which, having entered the bay from Bass Strait, would run up the river to spawn. He and his father, or occasionally his grandfather, had spent many winter evenings watching the net strung across a bend in the river, each bump indicating an eel struggling below. They would haul in the net, heavy with a twisting mass of eels. Each one was a struggle to release from the net although a quick tap with the ebony ruler soon knocked the fight out of them. Bled over the side immediately and into the hessian bags, the catch was reliable and relatively easy. One night the net was much heavier than before. It took the two of them to haul it in. "A log or ball of weed," he observed to his grandfather. The old man said nothing, grimly hauling in the net. The torch revealed the head and torso of a man, his waxy face partially covered by dark hair and weed, a neat circular hole in his forehead. "Turn off the torch," his grandfather hissed quietly. A razor-sharp bait knife cut the net free of the body and it slipped silently into the gloom. "None of our business," said his grandfather, glancing at the riverbank on both sides. "Get the net in," he said as he started the motor. They ran quietly downstream and out into the Bay. All the while the old man looking to the stern and beyond.

As they unloaded the boat, the old man looked at him in the dark and said, "You forget about that and don't you tell your mother or anyone else." "Never tell a living soul," he said fiercely. The next day they mended the net silently, it was never spoken of again.

Back on land they would salt the eels to remove some of the slime. His father or grandfather, as the case may be, would smoke them in a smoker made from an old 44-gallon drum over a small fire made from fence palings. Smoked eel was a favourite amongst the locals, and they made good money during the season. Sadly, while the eels were no doubt still running up the river, demand had gone years ago. No one fished the eel run anymore. He wistfully remembered early morning breakfasts with his grandfather at the Anglers Rest, the old pub on the river. The boat tied up in front of the pub, heavy with eels in hessian bags. The pub was now lost to the never-ending avalanche of yuppies destroying the rich heritage of pubs in Melbourne. A cheap meal of curried sausages with a cold beer was now forgotten, replaced by a restaurant pretending to be a pub and selling vegetarian tofu burgers made from some special save the planet tofu. He had a different reason for motoring up the Maribyrnong now – the "Warmies". The "Warmies" were well known by anglers as a source of a variety of fish. The Newport power station was at a bend of the river near the West Gate Bridge. Water which used to cool the turbines was thereafter discharged into the river. The unusually warm water encouraged marine life and, as a consequence, fish were plentiful. Salmon, tailor, mulloway, snapper, flathead and trevally could all be caught if you were lucky. This day he thought the tides and moon were right for mulloway in the river, they were often to be found hanging about in the deep holes near the Warmies. On the way he stopped at the remnants of an old jetty, black stumps like rotting teeth breaking the surface here and there. He cut the motor and let the boat drift silently in close to the old pylons. Moving stiffly in the early morning chill he draped a cast net over one shoulder and upper arm. With a rotation of his hips and a flick of one wrist the net was launched. It made a flat circular shape in the air, merging into a conical shape as it hit the water. After a few casts he had a dozen live bait fish, a mixture of small yellow eye mullet, salmon and tommy rough. Any one of them almost irresistible to hungry mulloway. They swam unhappily, circling in the large white bucket in the hold.

He carefully packed the cast net under the sharp end of the boat while it was motoring upriver toward the Warmies, the tiller roped midships. He carefully lined up the two marks, the house with the two chimneys and the channel marker with the red light. This was the spot his grandfather had shown him, over a deep hole on the south side of the Warmies. He eased the anchor quietly to the bottom, hand over hand and looped the rope over a cleat on the foredeck. Mulloway were deeply suspicious fish and spooked easily. Moving as quietly as he could in the still dark morning, he carefully sharpened a 3.0 suicide hook with

Chapter 25

an old whetstone and rigged up a sinker and swivel to a 50 lb line on one of his grandfather's old wooden hand line spools. Each were eight inches in diameter, hand turned by a bloke in the next street, now long dead. The wood was cypress pine, light and strong, from an old tree in his backyard. He loved the look and feel of them, with his grandfather's initials burned into the side using a piece of dowel with a nail hammered into the end. Heated over the fire until it was red-hot, the nail used to burn the initials into the wooden spool. While the wooden spools were old, the line was new 50-pound monofilament, purchased from Hot Fill. The swivels were his grandfather's, heavy solid brass, as thick as a pencil, the sinker handmade and heavy.

Like a surgeon he eased the hook just under the dorsal fin of a yellow eye mullet, avoiding its beating heart and other organs. He lowered it quietly and efficiently into the water and checked that it was swimming naturally. Seemingly unperturbed, the fish swam in circles, tethered by the hook and line. He lowered the sinker over the side and gently passed out the line. The hole was deep, and it took a little while to reach the bottom, then he took a few turns of the spool to bring the bait up off the bottom so a fish could see it and hopefully eat it.

He repeated the process once more over the other side of the boat. No more or the live baits would swim into each other and tangle the lines. He put a rusty screwdriver into each rowlock and put the wooden spools over each one. If he was inattentive the line would peel off as the spool rattled around the screwdriver but would not go overboard. The sun crept over the horizon as he waited. He had lost count of the number of sunrises that he had seen. He watched as it silently rose over the horizon casting a bright sheen onto the water. He would often ask himself why he kept on fishing but never while the sun came up. The truth was he knew nothing else. The other truth was that he liked the solitude of it. He certainly never got tired of the sunrise. What he did not like was the effort these days of putting the tender in and sitting for long hours in the boat. His knee ached from the Vietnamese shrapnel deep inside. His back would start soon, a product of too many hours in the boat and too many cold mornings. The old days of fishing from dawn to dusk or through the night and into the day were gone. So too, the days of long runs to the Rip. In those days, he would troll for kingfish. He would criss-cross the Rip until he found the schools of kingfish. Circling the school, he would throw big silver blade lures tied onto his grandfather's hand lines. He would haul them in one after the other, big fat kingfish, five pounds each, shining silver with green flanks and yellow eyes. He would motor over to Queenscliff and sleep in the boat for a few hours, later selling the catch on the pier for good money. He would repeat the process on the way back to Port Melbourne, selling the fish on the pier. The money was good in those days, but the hours and work were brutal. A young man's job, no longer for him.

He sat with one of the lines between thumb and forefinger of his hand, the other under his foot, alert for any touch on the bait. Occasionally, the line would vibrate just a little, the baitfish trying to shake off the irksome hook. His forefinger was protected by a length of bicycle inner tube, in case the fish made a fast run. Just like his grandfather had shown him. He smiled at the thought of the old man. At once, one of the lines started to vibrate in his hand. The baitfish was agitated, no doubt by an approaching predator. The Fisherman froze, waiting to feel the tension on the line. The line went heavy and tight in his hand and then shot away. Mulloway, like many fish, will take a bait and run with it before swallowing. Strike too early and the bait will be yanked from the fish's mouth. He waited. The line went dead and then was loose.

"Bastard," he said grimly hauling in the line. The lifeless baitfish, crushed from the jaw of the fish, hung loosely on the hook. "Tasted the hook and spat it out. Bastard."

He swore loudly and profusely but was encouraged. It had been a good fish which meant they were down deep and hungry. Several times more the fish went with the bait but did not eat it, a classic sign of big mulloway. Finally, he set the hook and the line tore his through his hands. He started an even-handed retrieve, slow and steady. Letting the fish have several, increasingly shorter, runs. The line finally came to the side of the boat, heavy and dark in the gloom. The fish broke the surface and rolled over, its huge belly flashing in the dawn. The gaff slipped through the lower jaw and he lifted it into the boat. Deep green and black flanks with big silver scales, the fish flapped weakly and flared its gills one last time before he slit its throat and bled it over the side. He would get at least $200 for it from a flash restaurant. It would pay for diesel, and food, for a week or two.

Chapter 25

After a few more runs from smaller fish with no hook ups, he pulled in the lines and turned the boat downstream. He was in the tender with the fish in the hessian bag before the Port Melbourne yuppies had had their first soy milk turmeric latte of the morning. Not a bad day out.

As he motored quietly down the river, he saw Jack, an eel fisher.

The Maribyrnong River had once been a great river, full of fish and life. Full of boats and fishermen. It had been in the lifeblood of Footscray and the surrounding suburbs, a waterway providing food, commerce and interactions in equal measure. The industrialisation of the district had been the death of the river, in so many different ways. It had become a polluted channel for industrial waste, far beyond the resource that it had once been. However, years of diligent quotes by activists had transformed the river and it was once again productive for fishing, albeit not like it had once been.

The Fisherman cut the motor and drifted quietly over to the other boat in the predawn fog. The old wooden boat had "X19" painted on its bow in faded house paint. On the stern, also on house paint, was "KIKINI" together with a faded decal of a topless young woman in a hula skirt. Jack had told him once that it meant "little girl" in Hawaiian. Jack had never been to Hawaii but intended to visit one day, he said. The boat was powered by a Seagull outboard, a variety seldom seen for decades. It was a small outboard motor with a petrol tank the size of a beer can and an open flywheel on top. The motor was started by an old piece of rope coiled around the flywheel and pulled hard. Mostly it started, albeit with some effort, but once it was going it was a quiet and efficient motor. It was all old Jack could afford. Jack had been fishing for eel in the river since before the war. He had been a friend of his grandfather's, and his father also. Jack was a man of few words and even less teeth. He fished from a wooden boat of about 17 feet in length, a mackerel boat as he described it. The origins of the boat were lost in the antiquity of the river. Jack had been fishing the river for eels since he was a boy. His father and grandfather before that.

The glory days of eel fishing, such as they were, had expired long ago. Jack had served five years in New Guinea and after the war had returned to eel fishing. It was good in the post-war years when money and food was scarce. Customers still had the taste for eel whether smoked or not and business was brisk. He lived in an unpainted shack on a bend in the river, in which his father and grandfather had lived. The shack was rich in history, dust and the smell of smoked eel.

Jack would catch the eels in nets woven by his father or grandfather, or in pots which he had made from chicken wire and reinforcing rods. He had been married briefly when he returned from the war, but it did not work out. His then wife finally becoming tired of his night-time restlessness and sleep talking. They had parted company on good terms, and he had continued eel fishing, the only thing which he knew.

Now, decades later, he was the last eel fisher on the river.

"G'day," said Jack.

"G'day," said the Fisherman.

"Getting any?" asked the Fisherman.

"A few," said Jack, the hessian sacks behind him large and moving like sacks of eels, which of course they were.

"Warmies?" asked Jack.

"Yep," said the Fisherman.

"Going for Mulloway?" asked Jack.

"Yep," said the Fisherman.

"Stop by for some smoked eel if you are around," said Jack.

"Don't mind if I do," said the Fisherman.

The conversation complete, they each went their own way, disappearing into the fog in different directions.

Chapter 26

The fish restaurant

He drove the Kingswood, recently quite noisy due to a hole in the muffler, to a former pub now a seafood restaurant pretending to be a pub. The mulloway in a hessian bag full of ice. Once one of the toughest pubs in Port Melbourne now it was a place for fat blokes in suits to eat overpriced fish and drink Barossa Riesling by the bucketload. Frank, the proprietor, was not a bad bloke but he knew fish like the back of his hand, having had several fish restaurants before. The Fisherman took any premium fish to him, knowing that he would get a fair price and no arguments.

He could have taken the fish to Angelo the old Greek fishmonger at the South Melbourne markets. Angelo was as mean as cat's piss and twice as unpleasant. He only dealt with Angelo if the seafood restaurant would not take a premium fish. The restaurant proprietor, Frank, looked at the fish and offered him a good price. He knew a good fish when he saw one.

"The Warmies?" he asked.

"Maybe," said the Fisherman.

"It is a river fish," said Frank, noting the dark green on its flanks. "It will be the top fish on the menu today," he said, handing the Fisherman several crisp notes.

"What else do you have?" enquired Frank.

"Nothing as good as this," said the Fisherman, the half-truth falling easily from his lips.

"Shame," Frank replied.

"What about some garfish?" the Fisherman asked, he had seen a few around and knew at this time of year they would school up as the moon got brighter. Restaurants love garfish, they look good on the plate, just like little marlin. They ate well but were not worth the effort of picking through the small bones in the Fisherman's view, but he did not care. Restaurants would pay through the nose for them especially large local ones. Frank's eyes lit up immediately.

"Shit yeah," he exclaimed, "Got any?"

"Leave it to me," said the Fisherman quietly, he liked Frank to think that he could produce fish to order. In fact, the truth was far different but as far as garfish were concerned, they were relatively plentiful at this time of year.

The restaurant was about the only place where he could sell garfish, but they fetched a good price. The only problem was that Frank was way too choosy with them. Because they were cooked and served whole, only the best were acceptable. Any damage to the beak or fins meant they were rejected. This meant for every five fish which were caught, probably two or three were rejected. Nonetheless, it was still not bad money. If Frank did not want them, he could often sell them to Bill the Younger. If not, he and Oleg would cook them on Oleg's wood barbecue

He spent the afternoon making gang hooks for kingfish and salmon. Using needle pliers and a screwdriver he carefully opened the eye of the long shanked 2.0 hook and threaded the barbed end of a second hook through it. The pliers closed up the eye of the first hook. He made gangs of three or four hooks to be used with mullet of various sizes as bait. To each gang of hooks, he crimped a piece of plastic-coated stainless-steel wire, about one metre in length. The wire trace would prevent the kingfish from biting through the line.

He ate the last of Ken's sausages for dinner, grilled in the old upright stove in the kitchen, spitting madly and filling the room with blue smoke. After two fingers of scotch and half an hour of some stupid quiz show on the ABC, he was in bed and asleep. The lath and plaster walls vibrating in harmony with gargantuan snores.

In the morning he would fix the hole in the muffler with muffler putty and some fibreglass bandage, as he had done so often. The muffler was largely made of muffler putty and fibreglass these days. As his grandfather would have said, "Plenty more life in it yet!" Indeed there was.

His grandfather fixed everything with wire, string, two pack glue or oil spray. Often with all of the above. If it could not be fixed with one of these things or a combination thereof, usually all in serious cases, then it was officially broken.

"This damned thing is broken," he would say, sadly. His grandfather hated waste.

Chapter 27

The fisheries inspector

Harry was the Fisheries and Game inspector. He had a brown uniform two sizes too small and a shiny white boat, two sizes too big. The uniform reflected his dull brown character, unlike the boat. The boat was over built, overpowered and had every gadget that you could think of. It had GPS, radar, sonar, radio, underwater TV and a small chemical toilet. It had a stove, a microwave and a sink. It was better equipped than Harry's one-bedroom flat, which is why he spent so much time on it. The table converted into a bed. Mai, his Vietnamese girlfriend, would visit him sometimes. She liked the boat. His wife did not, that was a good thing.

The Fisheries Department did not fit out boats like that normally, the reason for this fit out was Ronnie. Ronnie was Harry's first cousin on his mother's side. Ronnie was also the financial controller of the Southern Port Phillip Bay Economic Unit, as the Department called the upper reaches of the Bay together with the lower reaches of all the rivers which fed into it, mainly the Maribyrnong, the Patterson and the Yarra. Such was public service nomenclature, no one understood it except career public servants. They spent their entire working lives devising such policies and descriptions. It made their work impenetrable, so no one else would understand it. That was exactly what they wanted. Ronnie had a lot of clout and he approved the expenditure. Ronnie was also on the take, just like Harry. It was a good relationship.

Harry had been on the take since he was a kid, just like his late father Eric. Eric Simpson had been the most notorious fisheries inspector in Melbourne. He would turn a blind eye to a kilo of snapper over the quota or out of season, provided there was cash involved. A shilling a pound had been the going rate, pretty rough when the market rate was not much more. His real skill, however, came in the 1970s when the drug trade started from international cargo ships. Eric worked out very quickly that fishermen were ideal couriers for drugs dropped from the boats. For a long while the Fisherman's father had a good working relationship with Eric, largely because he always caught over his quotas. Eric would ask him to do some night runs and pick up parcels, in return for over catching the quotas. Such was life in Port Melbourne in the 1960s and 1970s, quotas were guidelines more than enforceable catch limits. As far as Eric was concerned, it was good to have a friend like Eric. Eric was not a bloke to say no to. No fisherman could take the risk of losing his licence and so Eric had plenty of accomplices. Harry had simply continued the family tradition, if not business. Eric prospered, so did Ronnie. They both bought houses on the Esplanade at Port Melbourne. They liked the view.

He heard Harry shuffling and wheezing as he made his way down the driveway long before he materialised at the doorway of the shed. Harry was a lifelong smoker, just like his late father. He started smoking when he woke in the morning and was at it all day long. It left him with nicotine stained fingers and a nasty cough which would double him over. He had such a coughing fit as he walked into the shed. When it was over, his face was white, his lips purple and flecked with yellow spit.

The Fisherman was busy sharpening bait knives on his grandfather's whetstone. He stopped and looked up.

"You don't look too good," said the Fisherman.

"Get fucked," wheezed Harry, putting a hand on to the doorframe to steady himself.

"I am concerned about your health," said the Fisherman solicitously.

"Piss off," growled Harry. Harry was a deeply unpleasant fellow both in disposition and in appearance. He had spent a lifetime working on both, but not in a good way. The only reason he had not been run over at the boat ramp was because there were too many witnesses, although the Fisherman suspected none of them would remember anything when interviewed by the police subsequently.

The Fisherman waited for Harry to regain his breath and composure. There was no need to say anything more, they both knew why Harry was there. Harry visited the shed every month like clockwork, ostensibly to review fish in the freezer and check for legal size limits. Harry never bothered checking the size and bag limits at the boat ramp or on the water because he knew that all the Fisherman did not have cash or sufficient cash in their wallets when on the water. In any event, it was bad for business, Harry's business, if he caught them with undersize fish or a catch in excess of the bag limit. He would visit them at their sheds or when they were drinking at the pub. He usually visited the Fisherman at his shed because it was private.

"Wondering if you like to make a donation to the Seamans mission again," he wheezed. "The mission really appreciates your ongoing support."

"The fishing has been a bit slow lately and there is lots of that imported frozen stuff on the market," said the Fisherman.

"The mission needs ongoing support," said Harry, his eyes narrowing. They both knew Harry was not collecting for the Seamans mission, the money went straight into Eric's pocket or more likely was spent on Mia, his Vietnamese girlfriend. Mia had a fondness for expensive shoes and matching handbags. Harry's wife did not have expensive shoes and matching handbags but then again, she was at least 10 sizes larger than Mia and not at all friendly.

The Fisherman knew it was inevitable and produced the role of banknotes from his pocket. Eric reached out for it with his large soft hand with fingers like sausages and the money disappeared like magic.

"The in-laws are coming for dinner on Sunday night," said Harry. "The wife's partial to those spider crabs that get in the net. If you happen to get six big ones, that would be good. I could pick them up on Friday arvo," he added. Spider crabs in the net was a convenient euphemism for ordering six large crayfish, caught order and ready for collection on Friday afternoon.

"There's not many spider crabs running at the moment," said the Fisherman, who was beginning to get a bit sick of Harry.

"I'm sure I won't be disappointed," said Harry thinly. The last thing the Fisherman needed was an audit of his catches or a check on the size of the mesh in his nets, which they both knew was perhaps a little too small.

"Still I can do, six you say?" said the Fisherman.

"Make that eight'" said Harry. "Big ones," imposing a penalty on the Fisherman. Harry turned left without a word; the Fisherman turned to sharpening his bait knife with quiet intent.

Slackwater

Chapter 28

Greek Easter

Each Easter the local Greek orthodox community celebrated the rebirth of Christ with a "diving for the Cross" contest at the end of Station Pier. The young man who surfaced with the Cross would be blessed by the local bishop, Phil the Greek. Phil's name was not Phil the Greek, but he bore a striking resemblance to Prince Philip and so was known as Phil the Greek by the locals, in fact, his name was largely unpronounceable by the locals who were not Greek. Each year the Easter competition was won by the son of Angelo, the biggest fishmonger in the South Melbourne markets. Angelo had been a local identity as long as anyone could remember, unsuccessfully running for mayor on two occasions. What Angelo did not understand was that whilst he was well known, he was not well liked. In fact, most people considered that he was as likeable as a fart in a space suit.

"Angelo's son, Domenico, won the Cross diving… again" said Bill the Younger.

"Again?" asked Errol.

"Yep," said Bill.

"How does he do it? Is it the third time?" asked Errol.

"F-f-f-f-fourth," said Phil.

"Must be a fucking good swimmer," said Errol.

"A possibility," said Bill, and after a dramatic pause he poured another beer for Errol. "Another possibility is that the contest is rigged," he said.

"Rigged?" asked Errol.

"R-r-r-r-rigged?" asked Phil.

"Is there a fucking echo in here?" asked Bill the Younger.

"How do you know it is rigged?" asked Errol.

"Don't ask me that," said Bill.

"How do you rig a Cross diving competition?" asked Phil. "The Bishop throws it in the water, a lot of blokes jump in the water and one of them pulls it out," he explained.

"Maybe he pulls out a Cross, not THE Cross," said Bill, feeling mysterious and important.

" What?" asked Errol.

"W-w-what?" asked Phil.

"Stop the fucking echo," said Bill the Younger. "How many Russians do you know with an oxygen rebreather set?" asked Bill. "You know, the ones that make no bubbles underwater?"

"Oleg?" said Errol.

"O-o-o-oleg?" said Phil.

"Stop the fucking echo," said Bill.

"Sneaky fucking Russians," said Errol.

"F-f-f-f-fucking oath," said Phil.

"That means Phil the Greek is part of it," said Errol. "That's dishonest."

"It is not dishonest if the Church gets a big donation from Angelo," said Bill. "The church roof is about to fall in, a new roof costs a lot of money. I reckon Phil the Greek thinks God is okay with it."

"I guess so," said Errol.

"Why didn't Angelo just give a donation?" said Errol.

"Ask fucking Angelo, not me," said Bill the Younger.

"People would think he was a good bloke if he made a donation," said Errol.

"But he's not," said Bill.

"Good point, but people might think so," said Errol.

"Everyone knows different and anyway he wants Domenico to go into politics."

"Politics! Domenico! He can barely walk and talk at the same time," said Errol.

"He'd be overqualified for politics then," said the Fisherman.

"Angelo also wants to buy the property next to the church," said Bill the Younger

"The one with the old people's home on it?" said Errol. "What for?"

"An eight-story assisted living centre," suggested Bill the Younger.

"What?" asked Errol.

Chapter 28

"Because aged care is where the real money is, every old prick brings in government money, lots of it," said Bill the Younger.

"Shit," said Errol. "But Angelo sells fish, not homes for old people," added Errol.

"Yeah but his cousin runs a construction company, Hellenic Constructions," said Bill the Younger.

"That big mob?" asked Errol.

"Yep," said Bill the Younger.

"What is it with Greeks and fucking property development?" asked Errol.

"Dunno but they are fucking good at it, just look at the Parthenon," said Bill the Younger.

"Fuck," said Errol.

"F-f-f-fuckenoath," said Phil.

"Fancy a jaffle?" asked Bill the Younger.

A shiny chrome jaffle maker sat on the counter behind the bar next to the antique sandwich toaster. Anyone else would have ditched the sandwich toaster but Bill had grown up during the Depression and hated to waste things that still had some utility.

"Where did you get that?" asked the Fisherman. "Did your mates on the dock drop another container of Jap white goods?"

"No, those days are gone," said Bill sadly and with feeling. "Fucking enterprise bargaining killed a very good earner, big mistake if you ask me. It's a refund from Hot Fill for the watch. Top-of-the-line. This baby will make four jaffles of your choice, golden brown in six minutes," said Bill clearly quoting from the manufacturer's packaging information.

"Never heard of Golden Lotus Blossom brand before," said the Fisherman.

"The next big brand," said Bill. "Spaghetti or baked beans?"

"For what?" asked the Fisherman.

"The jaffle, mate, we have them in exciting new flavours," said Bill the Younger.

"Toasted sanga, cheese and vegemite," said the Fisherman.

"Fuck you," said Bill the Younger, making the sandwich.

Neville, the black labrador, was asleep in the corner of the bar. Neville belonged to Bill and was the current incumbent in a long line of four such dogs. All labradors. All black. All called Neville. An unbroken line of trust, confidence and support. Such are the traits of the black Labrador.

"Why Neville?" asked Phil one day, the dog lazily wagging his tail at the mention of his name, albeit half asleep as Labradors are want to be.

"Neville Bonner, first abo senator," said Bill proudly.

"Did you know him?" asked Phil.

"Nah mate, but I always liked him and what else would you call a black Labrador?" replied Bill the Younger.

Errol farted loudly and Neville shot out the door like a flash of black lightning. Labradors are like that.

"Neville!" said Bill loudly.

"What is wrong with that dog?" asked Phil loudly, not looking up from the form guide.

The Fisherman looked quizzically at Bill the Younger.

Bill leaned over the bar to the Fisherman and said quietly, "Errol has a few downstairs issues, a bit of incontinence, man's 93 after all. He is very sensitive about it. So, every time there is an incident, we yell at Neville… bloody dog has got a complex now."

The Fisherman nodded gravely. "Not much else you can do really."

"Neville is tough, he'll be okay," said Bill the Younger.

"Yeah," said Phil.

"At least that's what we figured," said Bill the Younger, spraying a sickly-sweet air freshener where Neville had been asleep but mostly around Errol. Neville reappeared sometime later, he seemed no worse for wear, although perhaps a little nervous.

Chapter 29

A job for Skinny

"Skinny wants to see you," said Young Bill handing the Fisherman a beer.

"What about?" asked the Fisherman, after taking a thoughtful sip of the beer.

"Dunno," said Bill the Younger.

"How do you know that he wants to see me?" asked the Fisherman. The Fisherman had done some debt collecting for Skinny when times were very tough and continued to do some from time to time. It was not his preference but once you did some debt collecting for Skinny it was hard to say no. Skinny was a man with friends in low places.

"Mumbles was in yesterday looking for you," replied Young Bill. Mumbles, an associate of Skinny's was often sent to invite you to come and speak to Skinny. An invitation sent by way of Mumbles was not the type of invitation that you refused. At one time, Mumbles, despite his scrawny physique, had considered himself to be an amateur boxer of some promise. He had lost most of his teeth finding out that he was completely wrong in that regard. His speech now was punctuated by lisps and drools which had earned him the epithet of Mumbles.

He finished the beer silently and left the bar. He eased himself into the Kingswood, reversed out of the lane beside the pub and cruised to see Skinny.

Skinny did business from a shopfront in a side street off Graham Street which had once been a small drycleaners shop. It had no signage and was populated by swarthy, unshaven men of Middle Eastern appearance usually wearing worn and frayed dark suits with waistcoats. They sat on plastic chairs around cheap Laminex tables drinking thick black coffee from tiny cups with no handles. They smoked incessantly either small dark cigarettes or from hookahs which bubbled and hissed. The room was dark with smoke and redolent with garlic and other less pleasant odours. The men played backgammon, read well-worn foreign newspapers and argued animatedly in foreign languages. Some read the form guide, greyhounds mostly. Most of the occupants rolled rosary beads constantly in one hand.

Skinny was of indeterminate Middle Eastern ethnicity, with nasty black eyes, a three-day growth and a nose which you could take shelter under if it rained. He had a preference for black suits and gold jewellery in equal measure. Jailhouse tattoos occasionally showed themselves from under his cuffs. His physique was thin and wiry but that was not why he was called Skinny. Apparently, it was a colloquialism derived from an unpronounceable Middle Eastern name. He was a dangerous and unpleasant man who oozed malevolence. No one was sure where Skinny had come from or what he had done. However, he seemed to have an interest in most of the illegal activity conducted in Port Melbourne, a not insignificant business.

Skinny spoke in monosyllabic heavily accented English. The conversations were usually short, blunt and commenced with a standard greeting "I see you." The conversation was terminated when Skinny said, "I have spoken."

Skinny always sat at the same table in the rear of the room with a small group of similar men. Skinny's table was flanked on both sides by tables at which sat much younger men with sharp suits and even sharper haircuts. They had the physique of boxers and an air of capability. They did not play with rosary beads, play backgammon or read newspapers. They smoked small cigarettes and drank thick black coffee. They were alert.

The Fisherman entered the room, the patrons glanced at him briefly, and returned to their activities. An Arabic radio station was playing music in the background. He had been in the shop before and they knew who he was. Nonetheless, one of the young men with the sharp haircut rose from the table glancing at Skinny as he did. Skinny motioned with one finger for the man to resume his seat, which he promptly did. Nonetheless, all the sharp young men focused intently on the Fisherman.

Skinny motioned for the Fisherman to sit at the table. Seconds after he sat down a thimble of the thick black coffee appeared in front of him. "I see you," said Skinny in his thickly accented English. The Fisherman

Chapter 29

said nothing but nodded. Skinny was not a man upon whom one wasted words.

"You know Jimmy Mac" said Skinny. It was a statement not a question. "Went to school with him, he lives two streets away from me" replied the Fisherman. Skinny nodded, he knew both those things and a whole lot more as well, including the fact that Jimmy Mac had been in Vietnam with the Fisherman and owed his life to him. The story was reasonably well known but was rarely mentioned by the Fisherman. "He will listen to you," said Skinny. The Fisherman said nothing.

At school Jimmy Mac was James McKenzie by name but referred to by all as Jimmy Mac including by the teachers. It was not until he ran for appointment to the local indigenous body that he decided that he was aboriginal. He became known as James McKenzie – Kneebone, saying that he was indigenous on his grandmother's side. The Fisherman did not know whether Jimmy Mac was aboriginal or not, probably no one did. At all events, Jimmy Mac became an aggressive aboriginal activist and capitalised on his newfound aboriginal heritage as often as possible. He had positions on local aboriginal bodies, followed by a short stint in local government. He was currently the chairman of the Port Melbourne Indigenous Land Rights Advisory Council and a member of the State upper house. He was influential. This was assisted by the fact that his cousin Bill was an advisor to the State planning Minister.

Skinny proceeded to outline, in short sentences, that Jimmy Mac owed him some money. The debt apparently arose as a result of Jimmy Mac's fondness for gambling. However, it was not the money that Skinny was interested in but rather Jimmy Mac's support for a property development in Port Melbourne. Skinny had an interest in an aged care centre to be built by Angelo the fishmonger on land next to the Greek Orthodox Church. Apparently, there were planning issues and also rumours of aboriginal archaeological significance. Skinny believed that Jimmy Mac would be the ideal person to make these issues go away in return for the gambling debt going away. Skinny told the Fisherman that he would be very glad of his assistance. Skinny was not a man whom you said no to and the Fisherman decided that one day he may need to remind Skinny of this conversation. He knew the conversation was concluded when Skinny said, "I have spoken." "Leave it with me," said the Fisherman, not really knowing what he was going to do but he did not want to disappoint Skinny. Skinny was not a man who took disappointment well.

The Fisherman knew exactly where to find Jimmy Mac, at the Port Melbourne Bowls Club, a few blocks south of Graham Street. Jimmy Mac was a regular at the bowls club for several reasons. First, his brother-in-law was the manager and Jimmy Mac rarely paid for refreshments if his brother-in-law was behind the bar. Secondly, Gorgeous George, Port Melbourne's best-known SP bookie operated from a table in the corner of the bowls club. Jimmy Mac liked to be close to the action and did not like the thought of his phones being tapped by some over eager anticorruption zealot. Accordingly, when Jimmy Mac was not in Parliament, which was most of the time, he conducted his business either as a member of the upper house or with his indigenous brothers and sisters from the front bar of the bowling club.

"G'day," said Jimmy Mac through a mouthful of parma and chips, the $10 special on Tuesdays. "Skinny wants to talk," replied the Fisherman. Jimmy paused at the mention of Skinny's name but recovered quickly and swallowed a huge mouthful of parma and chips. "I am very busy," he said, reaching for his glass of beer. "What's it about?" he added nervously.

"It's about the gambling debt," said the Fisherman ordering a beer from the bartender by sign language.

"I know, it's coming, I'll deal with it," said Jimmy Mac pushing his plate away, apparently losing his appetite at this point. "I'm working on getting a new grant for the council in the next session of Parliament," he added. "I could fix up Skinny then, no worries," he said quietly.

"I don't think that's the answer that Skinny wants to hear," said the Fisherman.

"I am the chairman of the indigenous council and a member of the upper house for the State of Victoria… Skinny will get paid," said Jimmy Mac, his voice going up several octaves.

"Then you tell him that," said the Fisherman.

"There is no need to be like that," said Jimmy Mac.

"This is not going away," responded the Fisherman.

"This is racist," hissed Jimmy Mac.

Chapter 29

"He is asking you to pay a gambling debt Jimmy, that is not racist," said the Fisherman quietly.

"He is only doing this because I am one of the First Nations People," said Jimmy Mac.

"Skinny doesn't give a shit whether you are white, black, yellow, green or purple," said the Fisherman. "It doesn't matter what colour you are, you will bleed the same as anybody else if you do not pay the money to Skinny," he added.

"I think you're a racist too, you bastard," said Jimmy Mac.

"I think you're a prick," said the Fisherman finishing his beer and rising from his barstool.

"Just relax," said Jimmy Mac ordering two beers with sign language. "The thing is," said Jimmy Mac leaning forward confidentially, "I borrowed the money from the land council."

"Does anyone know that you borrowed the money from the land council" asked the Fisherman.

"Not exactly," said Jimmy Mac. "But I reckon that they might be able to look the other way if I point out certain other matters," he added.

"Would those other matters involve other borrowings by members of the council which are not recorded in the books of account?" enquired the Fisherman.

"Maybe," said Jimmy Mac visibly gaining confidence.

"So you could make that part of the problem go away?" said the Fisherman.

"Maybe," said Jimmy Mac, some colour returning to his complexion.

"But that wouldn't make Skinny go away, would it?" said the Fisherman.

"No," said Jimmy Mac, crestfallen.

"Do you know anything about a property development next door to the Greek Orthodox Church?" asked the Fisherman.

"Maybe, a little," said Jimmy Mac cautiously.

"There's problems with planning and maybe some indigenous issues," said the Fisherman.

"There might be, this area is very significant to my people, the First Nations People were here for thousands of years before you fellas," said Jimmy Mac. "We have a sacred bond with the land, and it represents all of our cultural practices and beliefs, it is a sacred bond," he added, quoting from no doubt a mission statement which he had written himself.

"I have reason to believe that Skinny would be very happy if the indigenous and planning issues were to go away," said the Fisherman looking Jimmy Mac squarely in the eye.

"Skinny?" said Jimmy Mac, "That is Angelo's development".

"Not entirely," said the Fisherman.

"Is Skinny involved in the development as well?" asked Jimmy Mac.

"Yep," said the Fisherman. "But not many people know that," he added.

"Well I sure as shit didn't know," said Jimmy Mac. "If I'd known that I wouldn't have put the sacred site ban on the site."

"What do you mean?" asked the Fisherman.

"That fat prick Angelo sat on the stool that you're sitting on now and asked for my help in relation to a different issue in relation to the church land. He is a constituent and of course I said that I would help. My cousin is the principal adviser to the Planning Minister and I know them very well," said Jimmy Mac.

"So where did the indigenous issues come from?" asked the Fisherman.

"I told that fat prick Angelo what my fee would be, nothing special, just the standard fee and he told me to stick it up my arse," said Jimmy Mac. "I called him a racist, he said I was dishonest, something I found to be quite hurtful and he fucked off," he added.

"So there were no aboriginal heritage issues with the site?" asked the Fisherman.

"Shit no, it was a worthless piece of swampland that no one gave a fuck about, not even my people, that is how the church got it in the first place, it was shit land that no one wanted," said Jimmy Mac quite jubilantly.

"So you can make the indigenous issues go away?" asked the Fisherman.

Chapter 29

"Fuck yeah," said Jimmy Mac motioning for two more beers.

"What about the planning problems?" asked the Fisherman.

"Fuck yeah ... That only happened because I spoke to my cousin about what a prick Angelo was being and that he did not want to pay us our usual fee," said Jimmy Mac triumphantly. "So if I do all this, the gambling debt goes away?" asked Jimmy Mac, his eyes narrowing.

"If you deliver then the gambling that will go away," said the Fisherman.

"Consider it done, thanks mate, I was in a tight spot, and there is an election coming up in six months, this would not have been good," said Jimmy Mac calling for two more beers. "Any time you need a favour do not hesitate to ask me," he added.

"Just make sure the issues go away, you do not want to disappoint Skinny," said the Fisherman.

"No worries mate, I am a man of my word," said Jimmy Mac and drank the glass of beer in one gulp. "Another one?", "That's my brother-in-law on the bar, these are on the house, I fucking love this place," said Jimmy Mac.

"No thanks, better go and have a word with Skinny," said the Fisherman rising from the stool and finishing his glass of beer here in the same motion.

"Give him my regards," said Jimmy Mac in his best politician voice.

The Fisherman nodded and left the bowling club happy in the knowledge that he was now owed two favours by two different people, it had only taken him an hour's work, and came with free beer.

Slackwater

Chapter 30

The stingray in the net

He set the net as usual, although somewhat deeper than he would normally set it. He wanted to try a new location, although he knew that it was probably a place where sharks and rays would frequent. He would like a few sharks, they got good money these days, but he did not need stingrays. They were nasty fish which would drag the net over the horizon before he could bring them in. Powerful, dogged fighters, who would not give up until the net broke or he killed them. There was nothing in between for stingrays. He hated them with a passion, as did all fishermen.

The net went tight, pulling the boat over as it did. The old windlass had broken down so he hauled it in, hand over hand, as he hauled the boat listed over toward the net. He reefed the line over the stern cleat, the boat listed even further. He used the cleat to help haul in the net. The net was a deadweight, sticking like glue onto the seabed. He knew what it was. It was not the biggest haul of fish in his life. He knew that it was a big fish but not the fish that he wanted. He knew it was a stingray. The problem was that the stingray would be tangled in the net. The worst of which was that it was worth nothing and it would destroy the net, or he would have to cut it loose. He could not afford to allow it to destroy the net. The other net had been cut up on a reef, when he was fishing a new reef trying to make some money. He did not have another net and had not had time to fix the other. He needed to get the stingray in close so he could cut it out of the net before it tore it to shreds. He hauled as hard as he could, using a loop over the cleat to improve his leverage. The net was a deadweight. It came in inch by inch. For every inch that he brought in, he lost a few more inches. He hauled with the line over his shoulder, one leg braced on the transom. Even then, he gained little.

After 30 minutes he was all but done in. He tied off the line and rested. His heart was racing but after about 10 minutes it subsided, and he felt better. He engaged the motor, careful not to foul the net on the propeller. I will drown the bastard, he thought. The boat picked up a little speed, weighed down by the heavy net and its contents. He was worried that the net would snag on a reef, and then he would be in even more trouble but the truth of it was that he could not bring it in on his own. He motored slowly over to where he knew the water was deeper and there were no reefs to foul the net. The boat was chugging hard, dragging the heavy net. He made slow circles, hoping that the stingray would drown. He knew that stingrays were hard to kill. He kept circling. He knew that he could not afford a new net. He knew that he could not sell the stingray. He had to kill it and salvage the net as best he could.

After a time, he felt that the net was heavier than before. The deadweight of the stingray was different. He hoped that it had drowned.

He brought the net up as much as he could. It was too heavy to bring over the side of the boat. He knew that there was only one thing to do. He anchored the boat. The chain was almost at its limit. He shackled extra rope onto it. He did not want the boat to sink while he was dealing with the stingray. He tied off the net, the boat listing badly as he did. He drew out the old sharkskin wetsuit from under the forecastle together with the webbing weight belt and black flippers. He found the face mask and snorkel, last seen many years ago. He hauled on the wetsuit, as he had not done for many years. It was stiff with age, hard and difficult to put on. His fingers hurt from the effort of pulling on the stiff heavy wetsuit. At last he was in the wetsuit, tight and stiff. Weight belt and fins were added as he sat on the gunwale, his back to the water. He found the old diving knife with its scabbard and buckled it onto his left leg, inside, like cave divers are want to do. This would assist in avoiding the knife tangling with the net. He did not want to drown with the stingray.

With a backward flip he rolled into the water, the shock of the cold took his breath away. He cleared his snorkel of the burst of air and after the bubbles cleared from in front of his facemask, he could see the stingray in the net. Black and huge, it was tangled in the net and his heart dropped. It was not the biggest bull ray that he had ever seen but he could not remember a larger one. It must have weighed 200 kg and the base of its tail was thicker than his thigh. The fish was motionless in the net and he set about cutting it free. It was hard work. For each breath that he took he was able to cut a few inches of the heavy lines which comprised the net. The fish was so deeply entangled that it was

Chapter 30

difficult. Every time that he went underwater was shorter than the last with his breath leaving fast, his strength even faster. He started to see stars before his eyes as he went underwater and knew that it was time to take a break.

After a rest he continued. Each dive was shorter than the last but finally he watched the stingray sink slowly to the sea floor, upside down and lifeless, white belly shining in the gloom. He felt a little sorry for the stingray, but this did not last. His net had a huge hole in it where he had cut the fish loose. It would take time to repair.

He floated at the back of the boat for a while, regaining his breath. After hauling himself back in the boat he rested again. Finally, he heaved the net into the boat. Exhausted, he motored back to the mooring.

He drove home, utterly drained. After a shower and some grilled lamb chops, he felt a little better. After three fingers of Scotch he was almost feeling normal. He went to bed early and was asleep within minutes.

Slackwater

Chapter 31

Painless

The toothache which woke him up was like a hot needle being driven through his jawbone by a sledgehammer. A handful of paracetamol tablets, only slightly out of date, did little to take the edge off the pain. The weather was drizzling rain and a stiff southerly had whipped up the Bay to white peaks like meringues. There was no point in going out on the boat and, in any event, he could not think properly with the toothache.

He stumbled into the Kingswood and drove to see the local dentist. The brass plaque on the gate of the rundown weatherboard proclaimed 'V.S. Bahattacharyya DDS (New Dehli) DDM (Calcutta)'. The brass plate was worth more than the house, he thought to himself. No one knew what the letters "V.S." stood for other than the names were as unpronounceable as the surname. Widely known as Painless, the obese Indian dentist was a pleasant enough chap, so far as dentists can be likeable. English was not his best language, nor dentistry his best endeavour, but he made do by poking around until the patient reacted. Then he knew he had the right tooth, or thereabouts. The surgery was accessed by a side door on the house which led into a waiting room with scuffed carpets, bad chairs and National Geographic magazines from 1954 to 1963. They had been bought by the dentist's wife, Binty, from the opportunity shop as a job lot – the whole box for five dollars. The old woman from the opportunity shop thought that five dollars was much more than they were worth, but she was happy to move them after so many years.

He had been taught how to pull a tooth and to fill a tooth, although extraction was far faster. His uncle also arranged for V.S. to get a handsome certificate in dentistry from his second cousin, Vinny (Vikrama was his real name but he did not care for it), in exchange for a nice second hand red scooter. It was a good deal. The certificate was resplendent with red and gold lettering. It was indistinguishable from the real thing. Vinny considered it to be some of his best work.

The surgery smelt of disinfectant and madras curry powder in equal measure. The dentist's chair was the same vintage as the National

Geographic magazines, resplendent in beige enamel and faded black vinyl upholstery. The other equipment seemed to be of the same vintage as the chair. Painless looked deep into the Fisherman's mouth through black plastic-rimmed spectacles with lenses like the bottom of a gin bottle. His eyes looked like a goldfish, darting around inside the frames. He muttered and made sympathetic noises between poking gums and teeth with a long sharp probe. "Does that hurt?" he would ask thickly each time he probed.

"Of course, it fucking hurts," said the Fisherman. "You are sticking that fucking thing in my gob."

It was apparent when Painless found the problem tooth, the Fisherman nearly bit off four of his fat fingers. With a pained expression and nursing four nearly severed fingers, Painless explained that the tooth could be repaired, although he would prefer to extract it.

"How much?" asked the Fisherman. The answer was a fee which was out of the question. The Fisherman was not flush with cash and needed what little he had for an overdue electricity bill and the last two quarters of council rates on the house. They agreed on a fee to extract the tooth, still quite a lot but within reason and available funds. Painless was well known to negotiate fees so long as it was in cash he did not care. Cash was important to Painless because he did not care to open a bank account. He would explain that as a cultural matter. In fact, his visa had expired long ago, and he did not want the attention that opening a bank account would bring. The tooth was difficult to extract but Painless got good leverage by using two hands and an elbow into the Fisherman's sternum. A few stitches and a mouthful of blood later, the Fisherman stumbled to the Kingswood and drove home. Painless had given him four little red pills in an envelope. They had Indian writing on them and he did not understand the directions which Painless had tried to explain. So he swallowed them, all with four fingers of Scotch. Soon life seemed much better and he was in a deep sleep.

When he woke it was dark. His head and face felt like they had been used for Collingwood folk dancing practised by elephants wearing concrete football boots. The little red pills had worn off somewhat but still managed to make him feel nauseous and he had blurred vision. In short, he felt like shit.

Chapter 31

"Fucking Painless," he said through gritted teeth. "Fucking hate Indians," he said. In fact, Painless was mostly Egyptian with some Pakistani undertones but the Fisherman was not to know that. He staggered to the kitchen, each movement causing a sharp pain and bright light from somewhere behind his eyes.

"Fuck," he said looking at the space on the shelf where the Scotch bottle had been. The last four fingers of Scotch had been drunk the night before.

"Fuck," he said again; with feeling. He drove the Kingswood slowly to the pub and staggered into the bar, drowning in a sea of nausea and pain.

"Fuck," said Young Bill. "What happened to you?"

"Painless," he said, spitting blood into a paper napkin which Bill had thrust into his hand.

"Fuck," said Errol into his beer.

"F-f-f-f-fuckenoath," said Phil, eyes like dinner plates.

The Fisherman grabbed the beer from Bill's hand before it touched the bar. He drank half of it in one gulp and gargled the remainder loudly, spitting blood into the napkin.

"Fuck," said Bill the Younger.

"Arsehole," said Oleg.

Bill poured three fingers of Scotch into a glass. "Ice?" he enquired.

"Plenty, some in a bowl too," mumbled the Fisherman. He downed half the Scotch and filled his mouth with ice blocks. He sat morosely at the bar, cheeks bulging, pink saliva dribbling from one side of his mouth.

Bill, ever helpful, put a straw in the Scotch class and refilled. "Mmmmh," said the Fisherman.

"Did you hear about Con?" asked Phil, eagerly.

"Mmmmh," said the Fisherman.

Con the Chop was a Greek bloke who had bought a car yard from Phil, after the insurance clean-up and payout. Phil had been keen to disappear and so had accepted Con's low offer much to his regret subsequently. Phil's car yards were strangely vulnerable to fires when times were tough.

"Could have sold it to a developer for a fortune," he would whine at the bar to no one in particular.

"You were lucky not to go to jail," Bill would say.

"Get fucked," Phil would reply.

"What about him?" asked Bill the Younger.

Since acquiring the site and business, Con had expanded his interests into rebirthing cars written off by insurers and giving them new lives, mostly on the Gold Coast where they were sold by his cousin Jim. He had a steady supply of cars, all written off by his brother, also called Jim, who worked at a big insurance company as a claims clerk. Occasionally, the cars were not entirely legitimate and sometimes the engine and chassis numbers did not exactly match. Happily though, no one on the Gold Coast seemed to notice or care. Even better, the local vehicle inspector was engaged to Jim's daughter Voula. It was a nice big happy Greek family.

"Con is doing a little porridge," said Phil happily.

"Really? What for? Chopping cars?" asked Bill.

"No, a little misunderstanding about the trust account," chortled Phil.

"Yeah that's the one," nodded Bill. "Any GST?" he asked gravely. Bill knew about GST problems having had several himself.

"A bit, not much," said Phil.

"Surprising, what did he get?" asked Bill the Younger.

"Two with a one," said Phil with a big grin.

"Not too bad," said Bill the Younger.

"He was disappointed," said Phil.

"He shouldn't have been, it's about right," said Bill the Younger, who knew something about such matters.

"Nah, he wanted more," said Phil leaning forward anxious to deliver the punchline.

"More?" said Oleg, who had been listening intently from behind the form guide.

Chapter 31

"If you had met his missus, you'd understand," warbled Phil, happy to deliver the obvious punchline.

"Right," said Oleg, not really understanding.

"Mmmmh" said the Fisherman, motioning for a top up and more ice in the bowl. Bill the Younger obliged on both counts.

"Couldn't happen to a more deserving bloke," said Bill the Younger.

"Fucker," said Errol.

"F-f-f-fuckenoath," said Phil.

"Arsehole," said Oleg.

"Mmmmh," said the Fisherman.

They went back to nursing their drinks and half-watching the Doomben trots on the TV above the bar. The man entered the bar quietly. He was short, lean and walked lightly on his feet. The shiny suit was tight, but it could not hide his tightly muscled frame. Tattoos in Cyrillic script adorned the back of each hand. He strode into the bar with an air of purpose if not menace. He could have been Oleg's younger, fitter brother although the Fisherman knew that Oleg had no family. At least that is what Oleg had told him once. Errol stared blindly at the door. Phil eyed the man warily. The Fisherman observed him coldly, he had seen many men like this when he was in Vietnam. Soulless killers who were capable of anything. Oleg folded his newspaper placed it on the bar and put his hands on his thighs. His eyes never left the tattooed man.

The tattooed man only had eyes for Oleg. He walked up to Oleg, ignoring everyone else in the bar. He spoke rapidly and quietly to Oleg only. The Fisherman assumed that the language was Russian, but it could equally have been Ukrainian, Siberian, or Martian for all he knew. Oleg clearly understood and fixed the tattooed man with a steely gaze on his stony face. In reply, Oleg spat a few words to the tattooed man. In return, the tattooed man became more menacing, punctuating his last remark by poking Oleg in the chest with a thick tattooed forefinger.

The onlookers would later say that they did not see Oleg move at all. Before they realised, the tattooed man was facing the other way with his hand and forefinger still extended, tight up behind his shoulder blade, Oleg forcing the arm up higher. The tattooed man went grey with pain,

Oleg whispering in his ear. Oleg then propelled the tattooed man out of the door into the night. Oleg returned to his seat and quietly unfolded his newspaper as if nothing happened.

"Fuck," said Bill the Younger.

"Fucker," said Errol.

"F-f-fuckenoath" said Phil, his face as white as a sheet. The Fisherman said nothing but looked thoughtfully at Oleg.

"Friend of yours?" asked Bill the Younger.

"Never seen him before," said Oleg, in his best Arnold Schwarzenegger accent.

"Well he seemed to fucking know who you were," said Phil.

"He called you Vladimir," said the Fisherman.

"He must've confused me with some prick called Vladimir," said Oleg.

"Where did you learn how to do that ninja thing with his arm?" asked Bill.

"TV," said Oleg.

"Fuck," said Bill the Younger, pouring another round for everyone.

Silently they watched a replay of the afternoon races at Randwick.

By the third race it was getting late, already past closing time, not that Bill the Younger felt constrained by such matters.

"Time gentlemen," said Bill the Younger in the approved manner, albeit a few hours after the real statutory time.

"Give us a hand Phil, would you?" he asked, motioning to the glasses and dishwasher.

"Right," said Phil, sliding out of his seat.

The Fisherman nudged Errol, snoring loudly on his stool.

"Time to go home old fella," he said.

He helped Errol off the barstool. He was feeling better now although his jaw and head felt like roadkill. "Give me a hand Oleg, we need to take Errol next door and then you can drive," he said.

The Fisherman was not unusually precious about drink-driving, but he had trouble focusing his eyes. Oleg had no driver's licence, but he drove well, in the Russian type of way, not much indication with turns and he preferred the centre of the road. Oleg put his arm around Errol's shoulder and assisted him from the bar, Errol's feet occasionally touching the floor. The Fisherman followed, albeit unsteadily.

"See you Bill," he said over his shoulder.

"Not if I see you first," replied Bill the Younger.

"F-f-fuckenoath," added Phil. "T-tell that f-f-fucken R-r-r-r-ussian never to come back," he added.

"Which one?" said the Fisherman, looking at Oleg. They found Errol's keys in his pocket and walked him into the rundown single fronted terrace two houses down the street. The hall was dimly lit and smelled of mildew. The Fisherman knew the smell was musty old newspapers because the hall was full of them, neatly stacked and tied in bundles. Yellowed headlines visible in the gloom.

"Shit, Errol what's with the papers?" asked the Fisherman. Errol did not respond, being well asleep by this stage, slumped into Oleg's shoulder. They found a bed in the first room, Oleg lifting Errol like a child and depositing him on the grubby crochet rug, wild with colours.

Leaving the key on the bedside table they left, shutting the front door quietly behind them.

Slackwater

Chapter 32

The incident in the lane

"The car is in the lane," said the Fisherman.

He usually parked in the lane between the pub and Errol's house. It was a dead-end lane which no one used. The reasons for parking in the lane were twofold. First, the now endemic parking inspectors could not give him a ticket, Bill had acquired the lane years ago as part of a council grab for cash. Secondly, the Kingswood was unregistered and had been for several months. Times have been a little leaner than usual for the Fisherman, although he was used to it.

The lights were off in the pub and the street was dark and quiet. No lights were to be seen in any of the houses. As they entered the lane, a tattooed man emerged behind them from the shadows like a ghost, blocking their exit. His dark eyes fixed on Oleg, he spat a few words at him. Presumably, the words were in Russian and presumably consisted of expletives. Oleg was unresponsive and impassive, his stance, tight limbed and tense, betraying an awareness of things to come, the Fisherman thought later. The tattooed man stepped closer to Oleg, repeating the Russian words with much more menace it seemed to the Fisherman. Oleg glanced at him and said a few words softly and presumably in Russian. The Fisherman decided at this point that if he intervened the situation may be diffused. He certainly did not want to stand in the lane all night, it was getting cold and he felt like a bucket of cold shit.

"Listen mate, no one wants any trouble," he started to say but stopped midsentence as the tattooed man spun lightly on his feet, a small shiny knife in his right hand pointed at the Fisherman's chest. Before the Fisherman could say "Fuck" Oleg exploded into movement. Afterwards, trying to piece it together, the Fisherman thought he saw two moves. The first was a blow to the tattooed man's throat accompanied by a tearing sound like wet Velcro. The second move involved Oleg twisting the tattooed man's wrist the wrong way. The hilt of the knife appeared in the tattooed man's chest, the blade deep inside him. The tattooed man did not make a sound, except for a gurgling exhale as he slumped to the ground. Oleg caught him and looking over his shoulder to the entrance of the lane, quietly rolled him into the shadows.

"Fuck," said the Fisherman.

"Shit," said Oleg glumly.

"Why the fuck did you do that?" asked the Fisherman.

"He was going to kill you," said Oleg, as if speaking to a child.

"I was negotiating with him," the Fisherman replied.

"No one negotiates with Boris," said Oleg.

"I thought you didn't know anything," said the Fisherman, who by now was feeling most unwell.

"He was Boris the Blade, we worked together," Oleg said quietly.

"Is he dead?" asked the Fisherman.

"What do you think?" said Oleg pointing to Boris's lifeless eyes, open and unblinking.

"Fuck," said the Fisherman.

"Fuck," said Oleg.

"What do we do now?" asked the Fisherman loudly. "It's a fucking dead body Oleg," he said.

"Fucked if I know," said Oleg in his best Arnold accent. "Put him in the bushes?" he suggested.

"How did you do that thing with the knife?" demanded the Fisherman.

"TV," said Oleg.

"Bullshit, where did you learn that?" hissed the Fisherman, trying to keep his voice down.

"I forget," said Oleg.

"Thanks," said the Fisherman quietly. "Do you really think he would have killed me?"

"Fuckenoath," said Oleg.

"Fucker," said the Fisherman.

"Fucker," agreed Oleg.

"We have to get out of here and take him with us. We will think of what to do with him," said the Fisherman. "Help me lift him."

Chapter 32

Oleg said, "It's okay," as he flipped the body over his shoulder and walked to the rear of the station wagon. "Open the door," he said. The Fisherman opened the tailgate of the station wagon, pushed aside the loose tools, rope and fish boxes and motioned for Oleg who rolled the body into the vehicle. The Fisherman drew a dirty tarp over it and closed the tailgate quietly.

Oleg rolled the dead man into the car.

"You've done that before," said the Fisherman.

"I forget," said Oleg.

"Stop that fucking forget shit okay?" hissed the Fisherman, by now feeling really bad.

Their voices awakened the occupant of the house on the lane, a light appeared in the window facing the lane a little way behind the front of the Kingswood.

"Shit, Mrs Kousoukas is awake, get down you idiot," said the Fisherman.

Oleg and the Fisherman ducked behind the tailgate and held their breath.

After a few minutes the light was extinguished.

"Shit," said the Fisherman.

"Fuck," said Oleg.

"Stop fucking yelling."

Oleg glared at the Fisherman in a Russian way.

It had started to rain heavily. The wind picked up. It had turned into a bad night and now had got a shitload worse.

"Let's get the fuck out of here," he said getting into the passenger seat.

They cruised slowly to the Fisherman's house, the streets dark and silent. Carefully, Oleg reversed the Kingswood into the drive and up to the door of the shed. It was 2 am and the night was black, clouds obscuring the moon. They sat silently in the Kingswood for a few minutes.

"What now?" asked the Fisherman quietly.

"Bury him," said Oleg.

"I am not burying a dead Russian in my backyard you dickhead," said the Fisherman. "It is the first place they will look, and they will find him."

"Not if you use enough lime," said Oleg helpfully. "Or acid," he added.

"Get fucked," said the Fisherman.

"Do you have a chainsaw?" enquired Oleg hopefully.

"No, and you are not using my axe either," hissed the Fisherman. "Where did you learn all this shit?" demanded the Fisherman. "Do they teach it at fucking Russian primary schools?"

Oleg said nothing, looking quite hurt in the dim light. "We can always dump him at sea," said Oleg. "Got any bricks?"

"Too many scuba divers and not enough sharks," said the Fisherman. "But there are big currents, that would take the body away. I know a place," he said slowly.

"In Port Melbourne?" said Oleg.

"Don't you worry about that, I know where to go, no one will ever find this prick," said the Fisherman. Suddenly he knew what to do and felt much better at the same time. "Help me with him," he said to Oleg.

"I will get him," said Oleg. He walked to the rear of the Kingswood and flipped the body, still under the tarpaulin over his shoulder effortlessly. The Fisherman motioned for him to follow into the old shop. He quickly emptied one of the big freezers.

"Stick him in here," he said to Oleg. Oleg rolled the body over the edge of the chest freezer and arranged the tarpaulin over the unseeing eyes of Boris the Blade. The Fisherman stacked the bags of bait and various fillets of fish over the top of the body. They closed the lid quietly.

"There," said the Fisherman. "No one will find the fucker. You and I are going for a little trip tomorrow night," he said to Oleg.

"Okay," said Oleg. He turned to leave but stopped and turned to look the Fisherman in the eye. "I can never go back."

"To the pub? Don't worry. Bill doesn't mind, provided you never tell him," said the Fisherman.

"My country," said Oleg. "I can never go back."

Chapter 32

"Don't worry, you won't have to, see you here tomorrow night at about 12 midnight," said the Fisherman.

The rain and wind had come up dramatically over the last few hours, as the report had predicted.

The Fisherman was worried about whether he could make the run down the Bay.

"Okay," said Oleg as he silently left into the dark. After Oleg had slipped away into the dark, the Fisherman carefully locked the shed door and went into the house. He was asleep before he hit the pillow. It was 4:30 am.

Slackwater

Chapter 33

The next day

He woke early as was his habit. He felt like shit but all things being equal he decided things were not so bad. He was alive, the bloke who tried to kill him was in the freezer and Oleg would never say a word to anybody. Things could be a lot worse, he decided.

The wind was fierce, and the rain was worse. There was no way he could make the trip down the Bay.

He stayed inside all day mostly to keep an eye on the shed because but also because his head hurt whenever he went outside into the sun. He heated a tin of tomato soup and ate it with some dry toast. His jaw was really sore, and he ate on one side only. After lunch the phone rang. It was Young Bill.

"Thought you might want to know, a couple of shifty-looking dickheads were in earlier looking for Oleg. Don't know his number but I know he lives across the road from you. Maybe you should tell him. Different blokes they were, but they looked like that fucking bloke from last night. Same fucking tats. Rats with tats, just like the other prick. Nasty little pricks. Fuck' em. Fucking Ruskies I reckon. Told them I didn't know any Russian called Vladimir. They fucked off."

"Thanks, did you say they asked for Oleg?" said the Fisherman.

"Nah, said fucking Vladimir or fucking stroganoff or Romanov or some stupid fucking Russian name but I reckon they were looking for Oleg. How many Russians drink at the Sandridge?"

"Yeah, righto, I'll tell him if I see him," said the Fisherman.

"Coming in for a beer?" asked Bill the Younger.

"Maybe later, got to fix the net, tore it up on a reef, maybe tomorrow," replied the Fisherman.

"See you then," said Bill the Younger.

The Fisherman replaced the phone in its cradle, thoughtfully. He peeked through the venetian blinds in the front room. No one was lurking in the street, no Russians that he could see. Although he thought he could see Oleg's outline barely visible in the corner of the window across the road. He felt comforted that the surly Russian was across the road. He had a newfound respect for Oleg and made a mental note never to pick a fight with him.

At about three in the afternoon there was a sharp knock on the door. The Fisherman froze. He was sitting at the laminex table in the kitchen, a lukewarm coffee in front of him. The knock was repeated. He crept up the hallway and slid silently into the front room. He managed to look sideways through the corner of the venetian blinds. The young Asian man had a clipboard and a nametag with a telecommunication company logo upon it. The Fisherman decided that he did not look like a Russian hitman. He saw Oleg vaguely silhouetted in the window across the road. He felt sufficiently emboldened to open the door. The young man smiled brightly and started a well-rehearsed script about changing telecommunication providers.

"Fuck off China," said the Fisherman, interrupting the young man mid-chorus. The man was used to such behaviour and switched to an alternative speech. The Fisherman closed the door and stood sweating in the hall. He crept into the front room and watched the young man walking down the front pathway, closing on the way the gate behind him. Oleg's silhouette had vanished from the window. The Fisherman returned to his now cold coffee. He studied the tide chart in yesterday's newspaper. After a few calculations in his head, he sat back in his chair with a smile.

"Fucking perfect."

Murray the Cop loved food. Not fancy food but good honest takeaway food. He developed a taste for it in his early days, the good old days when a cop never put his hand in his pocket for anything. You only had to visit the fish and chip shop at lunchtime and Jim (they were all called Jim) would insist on a free burger or a feed of fish and chips. Those days were largely gone now, much to Murray's unhappiness but new opportunities had arisen. The emergence of the American fast food franchises with really cheap food was like the second coming for Murray. Even better, he did not need to get out of his car in order to get a feed. A sausage and egg muffin for morning tea, some chips for a snack a bit later, followed by a bacon supreme burger for lunch. Murray was a fan of American food. It kept getting better, all-day breakfasts

Chapter 33

were quite the "best fucking thing since sliced bread," he would often say. Recently, 'Five for Five' at Hungry Jacks was a "fucking bonanza". Consequently, Murray was a little on the heavy side, but it was quality food he assured himself, which makes all the difference.

Murray the Cop quietly pushed open the door and entered the bar. All eyes went to the door and immediately turned away. Murray did not come to the Sandridge often, he had been at school with Bill and Murray's father had played football with Errol's dad. He thought it was a professional courtesy to leave the Sandridge alone, as much as he could. In the 1970s he ignored the brisk trade in white goods and other electricals in the front bar. In the 1980s he ignored the strippers until Mrs Koutsoukis had complained in person to his sergeant. In the 1990s he had turned a blind eye to the raffles, until Phil tried to raffle a BMW of dubious provenance. Accordingly, it was with some surprise, if not apprehension, that Bill the Younger watched Murray the Cop stroll into the bar. Even more strange was the fact that Murray was not in uniform.

"G'day Bill," said Murray the Cop.

"Murray, what can I do for you?" asked Bill, somewhat woodenly.

"A pot if you don't mind," said Murray.

More than slightly puzzled, Bill poured him a beer making sure it had the recommended amount of head. He carefully drained the excess foam into the slotted grate behind the bar. He placed a coaster on the bar and set the glass gently on it. Before he could say "On the house," Murray slid a crisp $10 note over the bar.

"How's business?" asked Bill the Younger, the bank note disappearing quietly into the till.

"Not bad, a little busy this morning. A missing person, some Russian prick called Boris Medvedev. His mates have reported him missing. Found a rental car in his name around the corner from here. No Mr Medvedev. No signs of suspicious activity," said Murray, inspecting the beer intently.

"Maybe he is rooting his girlfriend," suggested Errol hopefully.

"Could be, but he is not answering his phone," said Murray.

"Maybe he doesn't want to be disturbed, because he is rooting his girlfriend," said Phil, always wanting to help the police.

"He doesn't know anyone in Melbourne. Flew in from Sydney the day before yesterday," said Murray.

"So what," said Bill, "Doesn't mean he doesn't have a girlfriend in Melbourne."

"Perhaps, but he flew in from Moscow the day before that," said Murray, helpfully.

"Right," said Bill the Younger.

"His mates said he was looking for a foreign bloke named Vladimir Kutchenko," said Murray.

"Never heard of him," said Phil.

"Have you seen Oleg lately?" asked Murray.

"Who?" asked Bill the Younger.

"Oleg the Russian, who the fuck do you think?" said Murray.

"Not for a while, I thought he was from Uzbekistan, that's different from Russia," said Bill the Younger.

"Yeah he's from Uzbekistan," said Errol.

"Right," said Murray, his beer untouched.

"Don't know where Oleg lives, do you?" asked Murray.

"Nope," said Bill the Younger. "Hardly know him, he doesn't come here very often," he added.

"Right," said Murray. "Let me know when you see him." It was not a question.

"Sure," said Bill the Younger, "But he doesn't come here very often."

Murray stood up to leave and, as if having a second thought, said: "Old Mrs Koutsoukis was on the phone to my sergeant this morning. She says she heard an altercation in the lane last night. Don't suppose you blokes know anything about that?" he said.

"No mate, quiet as the grave here last night," said Bill the Younger. "Isn't that right boys?" he said to the audience in the bar.

"Shit yeah," said Errol.

"F-f-f-fuckenoath," said Phil.

Chapter 33

Murray looked pointedly at the Fisherman. "Left early, in bed with a toothache," said the Fisherman.

"Right," said Murray, making his way out of the door.

"Fuck," said Errol.

"Fuckenoath," said Phil.

"Fuck," said Bill the Younger.

All eyes turned to the Fisherman.

"Where is that fucking Russian prick" said Bill the Younger. "I don't like cops in here," he added.

"Murray is not a real cop," said the Fisherman.

"Murray is as real a cop as I want to see in here," said Bill the Younger. "So you can stick it up your arse. That fucking Russian can fuck off. If he shows his fucking face in here again, I will personally throw the prick out."

"He's alright," said the Fisherman, "But I don't think he will be in for a while."

"How the fuck do you know?" asked Phil.

"I forget," said the Fisherman. "Your sandwich maker is on fire," he said to Bill the Younger pointing to the shelf behind the bar.

"Fuck," said Bill.

"Shit," said Errol.

"F-f-f-fuckenoath" said Phil.

A silence descended on the bar like a wet blanket.

Slackwater

Chapter 34

Murray comes to the house

He heard the footsteps up the path long before he heard the knock on the front door. There was a familiarity with the footsteps that he could not quite place. He realised later it was the familiarity that one has with a friend, particularly one that has a heavy footfall which cannot be disguised. He had been to school with Murray, played football with Murray, done things with Murray that Murray would rather not recall, knew Murray's wife before Murray had considered making her his wife, and everything in between. In short, he had grown up with Murray and they had stuff between them that was difficult to explain. But he was now Murray the Cop. It was a bit more complicated. He was in the shed when Murray knocked on the front door and he rather hoped that Murray would go away. But sure enough he heard the familiar footfall down the driveway and Murray was in the shed as he knew that Murray would be.

"G'day," said Murray. "No answer at the front door, thought you would be here," he added.

"G'day," said the Fisherman.

"How's the fishing?" asked Murray.

"Not as good as it used to be," said the Fisherman.

"You've been saying that for 40 years," said Murray.

"Well it's been fucking true for 40 years," said the Fisherman.

"It hasn't stopped you from making a living for 40 years," said Murray.

"What the fuck would you know," said the Fisherman. "You've never earned an honest living in your life," added the Fisherman.

"There was an altercation at the pub last night," said Murray. "You wouldn't know about that would you?" he asked.

"Nope, left early, in bed with a toothache, like I said," replied the Fisherman.

"Things happen at the pub," added the Fisherman.

"Nothing happens at this pub," said Murray. "A cemetery would be busier," he added.

"Well, I was there and I do not recall anything unusual," said the Fisherman.

"There were some blokes, Russians, who were looking for their friend, a Russian bloke called Vladimir," said Murray. "Does that ring any bells?" he added.

"I don't know a bloke called Vladimir," said the Fisherman.

"I didn't ask whether you did," said Murray. "Do you know a bloke called Vladimir, a Russian?" asked Murray.

"Don't know that I do," said the Fisherman. "What does he look like?"

"A Russian bloke called Vladimir," said Murray looking hard at the Fisherman.

"All Russian blokes look the same to me," said the Fisherman.

"I thought you said you didn't know any Russian blokes," said Murray.

"I said I didn't know a Russian bloke called Vladimir," said the Fisherman.

All the while the Fisherman and Murray had been talking, the Fisherman had been intently sharpening a bait knife on an old whetstone. The bait knife had been his grandfather's and the wooden handle was dark with fish blood and saltwater. Occasionally he spat on the whetstone so the blade had some lubrication. It was hardly necessary, the blade was as sharp as a razor and he kept it so always. Murray watched the Fisherman sharpening the blade intently and quietly. Indeed, he never took his eyes from the knife and made sure that he was outside arm's-length while he was asking the Fisherman the questions. For his part, the Fisherman never took his eyes off Murray and, in particular, never took his eyes off the bulge under Murray's left arm where he knew his police issued revolver was in its holster. All the while Murray was speaking, he was leaning against the large chest freezer in the shop. This made the Fisherman quite nervous although he was careful not to display his anxiety or so he believed. Murray was on guard as only a policeman with decades of experience could be. It seemed to Murray that the Fisherman was hiding something but on the other hand he knew the Fisherman to be a man who was not comfortable with disclosing anything to a person in authority. This extended to Murray notwithstanding that the Fisherman and Murray had such a long and deep history. In fact, as it

Chapter 34

occurred to Murray, it was probably all the more acute because of their relationship, which was so deep and extended for so many years.

"So, how's the fishing?" asked Murray, in order to keep the conversation going.

"It's been better," said the Fisherman.

"Do you sell on the pier anymore?" asked Murray.

"Not really, perhaps occasionally, people don't really want that anymore. They would much rather buy fillets of fish from the markets which had been sitting there for days in the water, they just don't understand quality fish anymore," said the Fisherman.

"Pity," said Murray.

"Pity," said the Fisherman.

"They were good days," said Murray.

"They were good days," said the Fisherman, quietly. The Fisherman continued sharpening the knife on the whetstone. Murray never took his eyes off from the Fisherman or more particularly the knife.

"So you didn't see any Russian blokes down the pub the other day?" asked Murray.

"Only Oleg, but I don't think he is Russian," said the Fisherman.

"I think he is," said Murray.

"Maybe," said the Fisherman. "But I wouldn't really know."

"So you don't really know him?" asked Murray.

"Not really, he's a bloke who is in the bar now and then," said the Fisherman. "I've seen him from time to time, but I couldn't say that I know him," said the Fisherman. "Is he in some kind of trouble?" he asked.

"I can't really talk about operational matters," said Murray.

"So, he is in trouble, never trusted him, all Ruskies are sneaky" said the Fisherman.

"I thought you said you didn't know him?" said Murray.

"Well I don't, that's why I don't trust the prick," said the Fisherman.

"I see," said Murray.

"I was thinking of going fishing this weekend," said Murray.

"I wouldn't waste your time," said the Fisherman.

"What sort of bait would you recommend?" enquired Murray.

"That all depends on what you want to catch," said the Fisherman. "Big fish or little ones?"

"Only the big ones," said Murray, looking hard at the Fisherman.

"The big ones are hard to catch," said the Fisherman. "You need to be really good to get them and get up early in the morning."

"I've been doing that for 40 years and I've never lost one yet," said Murray. "Got any bait that might be useful?" said Murray looking at the chest freezer.

"No, only a few sausages and a leg of lamb that Ken the Butcher gave me past its use by date," said the Fisherman, tightening his grip on the bait knife.

"I've heard that the big fish like sausages and are extremely partial to a piece of lamb," said Murray.

"No fish that I've ever heard of," said the Fisherman, looking Murray in the eye.

"If you hear anything about the Russian bloke, you might tell me, okay?" said Murray.

"Don't you worry about that," said the Fisherman.

"So I shouldn't use sausages and lamb when I go fishing?" asked Murray.

"A matter for you," said the Fisherman, "But I wouldn't recommend it."

"Got it," said Murray.

"See you around," said the Fisherman.

"Not if I see you first," said Murray.

Murray turned quietly and left the shed, moving nimbly for such a big man. He walked quickly down the driveway. The Fisherman stopped honing the knife from the whetstone. He could feel the sweat trickling down his back and down both legs. He leaned against the edge of the chest freezer, he felt uneasy. He turned off the lights in the shed, closed the roller door and made his way into the house. He felt nauseous. He boiled the kettle, placed a teabag in a mug and sat at the laminex table. He sat silently while the kettle boiled. The kettle boiled and then turned itself off as kettles are want to do. The Fisherman sat staring at the laminex tabletop after the kettle had ceased to boil. He sat there for some minutes. The minutes became tens of minutes. The tens of minutes became longer. He went to the sink and removed the glass from the drainer. He filled the glass with Scotch from the bottle under the sink. He stared at the glass of Scotch for a long time. The room became dark as the sun went down. He did not move. He did not drink the Scotch.

"Fuck," he said. No one answered. "Fuck," he said several more times. Each time with more vitriol.

It was late when he went to bed. He left the glass of scotch on the table.

Chapter 35

The frozen Russian and the run down the Bay

Oleg materialised at the kitchen fly screen door at exactly 11:30 pm.

"Fuck," said the Fisherman, "Where did you come from?"

"Across the road," said Oleg, slightly puzzled.

"Fuck you, don't sneak up on me," the Fisherman retorted.

"Murray the Cop was here earlier." said Oleg, "I saw him," he added.

"He was looking for you, you prick" said the Fisherman.

Oleg looked hurt and sat at the laminex table. He was dressed in dark clothing with dark work boots. They drank a cup of tea in silence.

"Thought Russians only drink coffee," said the Fisherman.

"I forget," said Oleg.

"I am beginning to think that what you remember about anything can be etched on ants' balls with a cold chisel," said the Fishermen.

Oleg looked at him with a furrowed brow.

"Let's get on with it," said the Fisherman.

They went into the shop, careful to work without turning the light on. Oleg emptied the freezer of bait and fish, leaned into the ice box and hauled out the tattooed man. The tattooed man was frozen solid, with his knees bent where they had been crammed into the freezer. It was difficult work. The Fisherman helped. They peeled his jacket from him, icy and stiff. The Fisherman threw it in the freezer, stiff with ice and blood. The tattooed man had seemed to become much heavier, and the cold hurt their hands. They rolled him into an old fishing net, and struggling with effort, put the tattooed man wrapped in the net in the rear of the Kingswood station wagon.

"Just like a bug in a rug," said the Fisherman happily.

"What?" asked Oleg.

"How long have you lived here?" said the Fisherman.

"I forget," said Oleg.

"Just get in, we need to get going." They drove out of the driveway and slowly down the deserted street; the broken muffler loud in the darkness.

"Ver are ve goink?" asked Oleg, doing his best not to sound like Arnold Schwarzenegger.

"You'll see," said the Fisherman.

The car pulled up on a lonely stretch of beach where his old wooden tender was upside down on the sand. Oleg looked at him. Oleg looked at the little boat. Oleg looked back at the Fisherman.

"I don't like boat," said Oleg, reverting to broken English.

"Bad luck cupcake we are going on a boat ride and I need your help. I cannot get rid of sleeping beauty on my own," said the Fisherman. Oleg glared unhappily at him. Russians are good at glaring.

Together they carried the net bundle containing the tattooed man across the sand and lowered it into the bottom of the tender. They pushed the tender quietly off into the dark night. No one had driven past and there were no late-night dog walkers or joggers. The Fisherman rowed quietly to the mooring, Oleg gripping the gunwales with both hands. It was more difficult transferring the tattooed man in the net bundle into the couta boat. Oleg nearly fell overboard, and the Fisherman skinned his knuckles. Using a bait knife, the Fisherman prised open the compartment under the floor.

Checking that no boats were nearby, and seeing none, they rolled the tattooed man and the net into the secret compartment.

"What's that for?" asked Oleg, puffing slightly from the exertion.

"It is for exactly times like this," said the Fisherman.

They squeezed the tattooed man into the compartment. He fitted easily. The Fisherman was about to close the lid when Oleg reached in and withdrew the Heckler and Koch pistol. Expertly, he checked the breach for a round, ejected the magazine and slapped it home in short well practised moves. Oleg looked at the Fisherman inquiringly.

"Some fish are harder to kill than others," said the Fisherman.

"Anyway, where did you learn how to handle a gun like that?" asked the Fisherman.

Chapter 35

"I forget," said Oleg.

"Right," said Oleg, tucking the pistol into the rear of his trousers.

They closed the lid to the compartment. Casting off quietly, the Fisherman hauled in the sail tightly and Molly moved quickly into the darkness. Oleg sat amidships, looking marginally better than in the tender. Molly picked up speed in a nice breeze and with the running lights off she was almost invisible. The quarter moon was largely obscured by cloud, breaking through only occasionally. The Fisherman was pleased things were going well. So far, so good; he told himself.

"You okay?" he asked Oleg, who had not said a word since leaving the mooring.

"Not so good," he said.

"Seasick?"

"Always."

"Watch the horizon," said the Fisherman helpfully.

Oleg looked into the darkness, a row of streetlights were barely visible along Beaconsfield Parade and there was no horizon. "It doesn't help," he said morosely.

The Fisherman did not get seasick and could not understand those who did. He had no seasick pills but found an ancient roll of antacids in the tackle box under the seat. They were decades out of date.

"Take two of these," he said, figuring Oleg would not know the difference. Oleg did not. Oleg ate four immediately. Within 20 minutes Oleg was vomiting loudly over the side, a mixture of antacid tablets, tea and a quite nice Polish sausage he had eaten earlier.

"Make sure you don't get any of that shit in the boat," said the Fisherman unsympathetically.

"Fuck you," said Oleg, wiping his mouth with the back of his hand.

"I thought Russians were tough," said the Fisherman.

"Get fucked," said Oleg

He knew the route down the Bay like the back of his hand, even though it had been some years since he had made the journey regularly. He kept far enough offshore so the boat would not be seen, but close enough so he could navigate by the streetlights along the shore. The dark hull and sails made the boat almost invisible. The Bay was shallow in the upper reaches but without shoals. He tacked back and forward making good progress. The weather was mild and the breeze was constant. It was quite pleasant and he almost forgot why he was on the water. Oleg's dry retching over the side helped him to return to business. He tacked past Frankston, then Mornington and soon was off the cliffs at Rye. The tide was against him but he was making good time with a steady breeze. No other boats were on the water, not surprisingly because it was too early for the recreational fishing boats and the government had all but killed commercial fishing in the Bay. By now Oleg was groaning in the bottom of the boat, there was nothing left to throw up, not even bile. Oleg was one very sick Russian. But not as bad as the other bloke, the Fisherman thought to himself.

Soon he was gliding past the Fort, the old military installation off Dromana, a low black silhouette between Molly and the shore. Before he could see it, he smelled Chinaman's Hat, the old channel marker now mostly a Taj Mahal for seals. He gave it a wide berth. Often recreational boats would anchor nearby in the pre-dawn hours hoping for the big snapper in the deep channel below. Soon he could see Popes Eye as a dark silhouette off the port bow. One of the few man-made islands in the Bay, it had originally been intended as another military installation like the Fort but never completed. It was an annulus of bluestone blocks facing directly out to sea through Port Phillip Heads. He reefed the sail a bit harder, he had made good time and needed to be at Quarantine Bay before the turn of the tide.

Oleg moaned, face down in the bilges like some animal. The Fisherman ignored him and tacked again.

Chapter 36

Slackwater

There were no shore lights now and he ran close into the north-eastern shore. A former military establishment, the bottom of the peninsula on the north-eastern side was now a national park, although parts were still off-limits because of unexploded ordinance. At night it was deserted and dark, just what the Fisherman wanted. At last he could feel the change in the water. It became calmer and he knew he was in Quarantine Bay. He loosened off the sail to slow the boat down and angled towards Corsair Rock, just inside Point Nepean. Quarantine Bay was a small area of shallow water no more than two or three metres deep just inside Port Phillip Heads. One hundred metres away from the tide and the current now howling past at between six and nine knots, enough to suck any small boat out to sea. The tide was still coming in and would continue to do so about for 30 more minutes. He dropped anchor and relaxed for the first time in the last few hours. He had made it in time. Oleg was moaning in a foetal position in the bilges. The Fisherman ignored the Russian.

The entrance to Port Phillip Bay is a narrow stretch of water about 3.5 kilometres wide, although barely one kilometre of which is navigable. Enormous volumes of water are forced in and out of the narrow opening four times each day. Twice in and twice out. The entrance is about 10 metres deep inside the Heads and then drops suddenly to over 90 metres outside. The massive water flow causes currents and whirlpools which are treacherous and often fatal. The Rip as it is called is one of the most dangerous waterways in the world. At most locations there is a period of slack water between the tides. It usually lasts one hour. There is always six hours between each tide, including one hour of slack water. Except at the Rip. The vast volumes of water keep flowing until the weight of water coming the other way overcomes that flow. Slack water at the Rip lasted between 12 and 15 minutes not one hour. Sometimes on a full moon and a spring tide his father had told him, the tide at the Rip would "skip". That is to say, there would be no slack water at all, the water would simply reverse its flow without pause. The Fisherman figured that he had about thirty minutes until slack water but only 12 minutes or so to sail into the Rip and drop the tattooed man over the side. Once the body was over the side it would be carried out on the tide into 90 metres of water and then far out into Bass Strait. No one would ever find the body.

He dropped the anchor and waited. Oleg sat up slowly, pale even in the darkness.

"Fuck," he said.

"About time, you can help," said the Fisherman.

"It is better when the boat does not move," said Oleg quietly.

"Great, help me with this bastard," said the Fisherman.

The tattooed man had not thawed out much and was still solid and extremely unmanageable. Together they wrestled him from the secret compartment and tied an old car battery around his waist with nylon rope. It was hard work and both men were breathless afterwards. The Fisherman scanned the Rip looking for any fishing boat or worse, a container vessel making its way through the Heads. Often they would wait and time the run through the Rip at slack water or on the incoming tide but not so tonight. Nor could he see one of the bright orange pilot boats rushing out from Queenscliff to shepherd a vessel in or out of the Heads. Perfect, he thought to himself.

Oleg, feeling much better, sat upright as the Fisherman set off, Molly gathering speed as she left Quarantine Bay and entered the Rip, Corsair Rock on the left and then they passed Point Nepean into the Rip itself. The boiling water subsided before their eyes, strangely black and shiny in the night. The Fisherman steered the boat across the face of the Rip until he was just outside the Heads where the bottom fell away to 60 metres and then again to 90 metres. This was Lonsdale Wall, the most dangerous place in the Rip. He tied off the tiller and sprang back to help Oleg manoeuvre the frozen tattooed man half over the side of the boat. The water started to boil once more, but in the opposite direction. The boiling of the water told him that the tide had turned and immediately had accelerated outwards through the Heads. There had been no slack water, just as his father had said might happen. The sail started to flap as the boat lost momentum, quickly it began listing in the wrong direction as they tried to heave the frozen tattooed man over the side. The body

Chapter 36

was stiff and heavy. The boat was listing and rocking violently with the tide and the exertions of the two men.

The body had to be lifted from the hold and then over the deck, which made it difficult in all the circumstances. When they were almost over and onto the deck the car battery suddenly slipped back into the hold and became jammed under the gunwale.

"Fuck," said the Fisherman.

"Fuck," said Oleg.

"Hold him," said the Fisherman.

"What the fuck do you think I am doing?" asked Oleg.

The boat was listing dangerously now and starting to accelerate sideways out of the Rip and into Bass Strait. It was moments from capsizing, realised the Fisherman. The boat fell broadside into a trough followed by a standing wave, two metres in height. The boat fell heavily into the trough, water cascading over the gunwale.

The Fisherman, eyes blinded by saltwater, groped for the bait knife which he always kept jammed into a space between one of the wooden ribs under the gunwale. He found it and quickly slashed the rope securing the car battery to the body. Free of the snag, Oleg, with a massive effort, rolled the body into the water. With barely a splash the body disappeared into the inky black water. The Fisherman darted to the stern and grabbed the tiller, throwing off the looped rope. He hauled in the sail and the boat picked up momentum, slowly at first. The water in the Rip was now a maelstrom of whirlpools, boiling sections of water forced up by underwater obstacles and the nasty chop travelling in all directions. The worst of the sections were waves two metres high, driven by some underwater cliff. There had not been 16 minutes of slack water or even 12, the tide had skipped just like his grandfather had told him. It had gone from one direction at nine kilometres to the other at almost the same speed and was rapidly accelerating with the whole of Port Philip Bay pushing the water through the narrow opening. The chop on the water soon became vicious, driven by the fast current travelling in the opposite direction to the wind, which had shifted in the morning cool. The Fisherman barely avoided a two metre high standing wave which had grown up on the starboard bow, out of nowhere. Oleg was too scared to be sick, gripping the gunwale with a face as white as a sheet, shining even in the black night. The boat porpoised over the chop throwing a sheet of spray each time it crashed into the valley on the other side. Molly drove resolutely on, the Fisherman's grip on the tiller like steel, the main halyard tight in his other hand.

Within a few long minutes they had crossed to the other side of the Rip and were in a calmer stretch of water, soon they were off Queenscliff Pier. The Fisherman exhaled for the first time in minutes, so it seemed. His shoulders slumped and he dropped the halyard through his hand. The sails luffed and the boat slid through the calm water. The Fisherman, Oleg and the boat were all exhausted, wrung out from adrenaline.

"Fuck," said Oleg quietly, but with feeling.

"Yep," said the Fisherman. "You don't get much closer than that."

"Is he gone?" asked Oleg.

"Too fucking right he is gone. No one will ever see that bastard again," said the Fisherman. Oleg wanted to laugh with relief but his ribs and guts hurt too much to breathe. They sat in silence, the boat gently rocking, the waves slapping the hull quietly.

"But the body had no weight on it,' said Oleg. "It will float."

"No chance," said the Fisherman. "It was like a solid block of ice. It will sink and get sucked out into Bass Strait," he continued. Secretly, he was worried, but he did not want to tell Oleg. He was just relieved that they had not capsized the boat and joined the frozen Russian at the bottom of Lonsdale Wall.

They sat silently for a while longer.

Oleg exhaled loudly.

The Fisherman exhaled loudly.

Soon they were laughing wildly, a post adrenaline let down fuelled hysteria.

Chapter 37

The run home

The boat rocked gently in the calm inshore water, a relief to both men after the seething maelstrom of the Rip. They sat in silence watching the sun climb over the horizon, colouring the water a deep gold. A few recreational fishing boats shot out from the harbour at Queenscliff, white and fast, anxious to be the first out for the day.

"Some blokes were looking for you at the pub yesterday," said the Fisherman.

"What did they look like?" asked Oleg.

"Like nasty fucking Russians," said the Fisherman, although he had not seen them. He felt the need to impress on Oleg the importance of the moment.

"Right," said Oleg, feeling much better now although his ribs hurt when he breathed.

"Maybe you should lie low for a while," said the Fisherman.

"Yeah," said Oleg. "I cannot go back," he added.

"I know," said the Fisherman.

"He came to kill me, he said I killed his brother," said Oleg.

"What, the bloke with the knife?" asked the Fisherman.

"Yeah," said Oleg.

"Did you?" asked the Fisherman?

"Yes," replied Oleg.

"Here?" said the Fisherman.

"No," said Oleg.

"Russia?" inquired the Fisherman.

"I forget," said Oleg.

"Right," said the Fisherman, unhappy at this point.

"I cannot go back," said Oleg.

"Because of that?" asked the Fisherman.

"Yes... No, other things as well," Oleg said hesitantly.

"What?" asked the Fisherman.

"I forget," said Oleg impassively.

"Fuck you," said the Fisherman.

"Fuckenoath," said Oleg in his best Arnold accent.

Oleg was silent and then spoke slowly and deliberately.

"There was a war in my country. I was part of it. Unfortunately, I was on the wrong side," said Oleg slowly. Things were done," he added. His English seemed suddenly to be more fluent, the Fisherman observed to himself.

"Now people want to chase those who were involved and in charge. I was in charge," he said.

"I thought it was right at the time," said Oleg, in surprisingly good English, albeit heavily accented.

"I understand," said the Fisherman. "My war was in Vietnam, but it was the same as yours."

"I thought so," said Oleg.

"Never tell a living soul about what we have done," said the Fisherman.

"Correct," said Oleg. There was no need to shake hands. The Fisherman knew Oleg was good for his word.

By now the sun was above the horizon and small white boats were zooming around nearby. Sails set, they ran with light breezes, tacking slowly up the Bay. The Fisherman showed Oleg how to run the lures out for kingfish. Oleg sat amidships looking almost happy, the Fisherman at the tiller. There were no container ships traversing the Bay so they were free to tack from side to side, in long slow traverses. Soon they found a school of nice fat kingfish and the Fisherman dropped the sail. Motoring around the school as it moved here and there, they caught enough kingfish to almost fill the hold. It was almost like the old days but not quite. The Fisherman dropped some lures below the school of kingfish hoping to catch a few big snapper often lurking below the hungry kingfish, gobbling up the scraps of bait fish overlooked by the fast-moving kingfish. Before long, he had four good snapper on board, dusky red with the bulbous forehead of the really old ones.

Chapter 37

The hold now full they ran up the sails and with the old diesel helping they were soon making a good pace up the Bay. Oleg seemed to get his sea legs on the return trip, only dry retching a few times when they hit a nasty chop. The Fisherman's jaw ached, his back was stiff and painful, and his knee hurt terribly. Other than that, he felt quite good, certainly he felt good having a hold full of premium fish. He tied off the tiller and started to bleed and fillet the fish. Oleg joined in, it was clear that he knew what he was doing and handled the knife with ease. Oleg worked quickly with a sharp bait knife, disembowelling the fish in good time.

"Where did you learn to use a knife like that?" asked the Fisherman. Oleg started to answer but was interrupted by the Fisherman. "I know… you fucking forgot."

"Old habits die hard," said Oleg quietly.

"I know, I've seen it," said the Fisherman.

"He would have killed you," said Oleg.

"I know, thanks," said the Fisherman. Oleg silently gutted a large snapper.

The Fisherman returned to the tiller, Oleg hauled up the sail and got the boat underway, forcing a powerboat to give way in the process. He felt good about that, although the swarthy fisherman in the shiny white fibreglass boat was less than pleased.

"Fucker," said the Fisherman.

"Fucker," said Oleg happily.

He had no ice on board so he was keen to get to the mooring as soon as he could. They were back in the tender by mid-morning, the fish in hessian bags on the floor. As they beached the tender, a few curious dog walkers idly asked, "How did you go?" "Not bad," said the Fisherman. They lugged the wet bloodied bags to the Kingswood. It took two trips. The Kingswood started noisily, the muffler loud in the late morning. They motored back to the Fisherman's shed, driving slowly into the street looking for nasty Russians. Seeing none he reversed the Kingswood into the driveway. They sat in silence for a minute or two.

"Better move this fish," said the Fisherman.

"Yeah," said Oleg.

"Maybe not a good idea to go to the pub for a while," said the Fisherman.

"Yeah," said Oleg.

Oleg got out of the car and after helping the Fisherman to unload, walked briskly across the road to his house. The Fisherman cruised to the fish restaurant and walked into the old front bar. He found Frank the proprietor wiping the blackboard menu clean.

"Just in time," Jack said. "Got those gars?"

"Nope, but kingfish and big reds." Now Frank was very partial to big snapper, he would display them on ice on the bar, shiny and red with a few sprigs of parsley scattered about. The punters would pay anything for a fillet from one of those magnificent fish, and Frank adjusted his prices accordingly. Kingfish were a good fish also. Frank wasn't his real name of course, it was Gianni, a Cypriot who had emigrated to Melbourne in the 1960s like so many others. His family had had a fish restaurant in Cyprus, and he thought to do the same in Australia. It took him a decade of working on the scallop boats in Port Philip Bay to accrue the cash for his first shop, a fish and chip shop in Fisherman's Bend. A few transactions and with the benefit of a cash economy, he had his first fish restaurant. Not paying tax was a real help with business management. Fortunately, he did well enough to buy the old pub and turn it into the establishment it was today. Years of working in the industry had made him crafty and shrewd.

"Any good?" he said cautiously.

"Fucking fantastic, just inside the Rip this morning. Still stiff, they are that fresh," said the Fisherman.

"Great, show me," he said. "The Rip? What were you doing way down there?"

"Hadn't been there for a while, thought I'd take Molly for a run, like the old days," explained the Fisherman.

"Just like the old days," said Frank quietly.

His second cousin, Con, actually Constantino, had been a merchant seaman who had jumped ship inside the Heads in the 1970s. The Fisherman had picked him up and dropped him off at a lonely stretch of sand between Fisherman's Bend and the mouth of the Yarra. Frank

Chapter 37

knew of this because he had brokered the deal with Syd the Squid. The Fisherman knew that Frank knew, but neither of them spoke of it. He saw Con working in the kitchen of the fish restaurant from time to time. Neither acknowledged the other.

Frank took a quick look, a poke here and a lift of the gill cover was all it took for him to make an offer on all the snapper. A good price too. The Fisherman hesitated, "What about the kingfish?"

After an inspection, Frank thought for a moment and said, "$350 for the lot." The job lot price was not bad, better than the snapper alone and he did not have to try and flog the kingfish elsewhere. "Done," he said.

"Outstanding," said Frank, "I'll write them up on the board now… straight from the Rip this morning".

He counted well-worn notes into the Fisherman's hand. They disappeared into his pocket in a flash, no paperwork, of course. Both men were happy, a good deal for each.

"Don't forget those gars."

"Righto, maybe in a few days, moon's looking good," said the Fisherman.

"Beer?" asked Frank.

"Maybe a quick one," said the Fisherman, realising he had not eaten or drunk anything since last night. He downed the beer in one gulp and after a quick farewell, climbed into the noisy Kingswood and cruised away. Life was good, if only for a little while, but who cared about that. "You wouldn't be dead for quids," his father would say. Well, he felt like it today. For the first time in a long time he felt good in himself, a pocketful of cash did not hurt either. However, the Russian business still made him uneasy. He took to looking in the rear-view mirror somewhat more than usual.

Chapter 38

Oleg says goodbye

The Kingswood burbled back to the Fisherman's house and he reversed it into the driveway as usual. He had in mind a shower and a shave before a light lunch at the pub. Afterwards he felt good and whistled to himself quietly. A knock on the door and he froze in his footsteps. The knock was repeated, this time louder. He crept down the hall and edged to the window from inside the front room. Peering through the venetians he saw Oleg, in clean clothes with a grubby duffel bag over his shoulder. He opened the door.

"Thought you were those fucking Russians," said the Fisherman.

"Going away for a while," said Oleg.

"Good idea, where?" asked the Fisherman.

"Eucumbene, … know a bloke up there, … worked with him on the Project," responded Oleg.

"Righto, … keep an eye on the pile of bricks?" the Fisherman inquired.

"Thanks," said Oleg.

"How do I contact you?" asked the Fisherman.

"I'll contact you," said Oleg.

"Righto," said the Fisherman.

Without another word, Oleg turned and walked briskly down the street toward the light rail station, presumably on his way to Spencer Street to catch a train to New South Wales. The Fisherman closed the door, fired up the Kingswood and burbled noisily to the pub. Errol, Phil and Bill all looked up as he walked into the bar. Bill the Younger poured a beer and placed it on the bar in front of the Fisherman's usual stool.

"Where's Oleg?" said Phil.

"Gone," said the Fisherman quietly, taking a deep draft of beer.

"Good idea," said Bill the Younger. "Where?"

"I forget," said the Fisherman. "What about them Ruskies?" he added.

"Haven't been back," said Bill the Younger. "We told them that we didn't know no Vlad. Mrs Koutsoukis was in here this morning whining about last night's noise in the lane," said Bill the Younger. "Don't know anything about that do you?" he enquired.

"Probably rats," said the Fisherman.

"Must have been a fucking big one with a fucking blood nose," said Bill the Younger quietly. He leaned forward so that only the Fisherman could hear, "Took me half an hour to hose all the blood away," he added softly.

"Must have been a big one," said the Fisherman. The Fisherman thereafter was deeply involved in a real-time study of the bubbles in his beer glass. He looked up to see Bill the Younger staring at him.

"What?" he said.

"Nothing," said Bill the Younger. "What about some lunch?" he asked.

"Good idea," said the Fisherman "I'm fucking starving, what's on?"

"Anything you want, what about a pie?" said Bill the Younger.

"Feel like a toasted sandwich," said the Fisherman.

"Speciality of the house," said Bill the Younger. "Get fucked," he added.

The Fisherman studied the bubbles in his beer glass. After a while he took his beer and moved into Oleg's seat. He could see both doors into the bar from this seat. He felt better, but not much.

Chapter 39

The singer in the bar

The next evening, he was feeling quite good and decided to go to the jazz bar in Graham Street.

Sometimes he would go to the bar. He quite liked jazz music but there was another reason. The reason he went there was the girl who sang in the bar. She was there every Thursday night. It was wrong, but flattering to call her a girl, she had seen too many moons for that. But he liked to think of her as a girl. She probably did too. She had sung with the local jazz greats, name anyone and she had sung with them either as backup or in front. But like all things, life had not gone to plan. She had spent time as a waitress, a grief counsellor and a disability support worker, none of which she liked much. But she had a regular Thursday gig and the owner liked her, a little too much for her way of thinking but it was a regular gig and the crowd, if one could call them that, were pleasant if not indifferent.

She had a set which included "Cry Me A River", "Black Magic" and a lot of others. She did not like singing anything else but jazz and even then, she did not particularly like singing cover versions of other people's songs, but the audience liked the songs that they knew. The less well-known songs, particularly her own, were the ones that she liked to sing and every now and then she had tried to put some energy into one in order to get the audience onside. It was hard work. It was far easier to sing the songs that they knew. The $5 cover charge seemed a lot some nights and the audience made their views clear. For his part, he thought that her version of "Cry Me A River" was better than Diana Krall in that "Live at Paris" record. He would often play it on the old record player in the front room of the house sitting in the dark with two fingers of cheap Scotch in a glass. During breaks in between the sets, she would sit at the bar nursing a glass of white wine and reading a book, Henry James mostly. He told her one night that he really liked her version of "Cry Me a River". For a moment he thought she would cry, but she did seem to appreciate his company. Indeed, she told him that afterwards in a flat which was off Graham Street. They sometimes ended up in her flat. He liked it when they did. The stage name was Crystal Diamond. Her real name was Agatha. She hated her real name. He quite liked it. When he told her that, she said "don't be stupid, no serious singer is called Agatha." He liked her name nonetheless, although she was very touchy about it. He assumed that all singers were quite high strung and prone to being difficult. Agatha certainly was.

The bar where Agatha – Crystal – sang was owned by a Croatian Muslim, Farouk Balharzi. Farouk was also called Freddie. Outside of his presence, he was known as Freddie Two Tooth, the reason being that he had very prominent front teeth just like Freddie Mercury but with a gap in between his front two teeth like the English movie actor from the "Carry On" films. If you saw the size of Freddie, you would understand why no one called him Freddie Two Tooth to his face. He was large, very hairy and sweated a lot. He would answer to being called "Freddie" but only from people he knew, and he considered himself quite handsome in a Croatian Muslim sort of way. At least he thought so. He considered himself a moderate Muslim of world proportions. In truth, he was a nasty, vindictive fat shit who liked nothing more than to short serve his customers and short change his staff.

His brother was the sergeant at arms for a local motorcycle gang and Freddie basked in his brother's glory every day. A little dealing in stolen goods and methamphetamine on the side helped Freddie keep the tax man at bay. He had a fondness for shiny suits in garish colours which he considered to be quite attractive, if 180 kg of hairy Croatian Muslim could be attractive. His fondness for shiny suits was only out done by a fondness for shiny gold jewellery. He had lots of it and made sure it was well polished and very visible. He considered it enhanced his natural beauty. Most people who knew Freddie did not share this view, and in particular, it did little to overcome more significant issues of bad breath and very unpleasant body odour.

The Fisherman sat in the back of the room, nursing a Scotch and feeling good to be alive, listening to Agatha.

In a break she came to sit with him for a while. She seemed happy to see him, at least he thought so.

"There were some foreign blokes in here earlier," she said. "Looking for a bloke called Vladimir."

"What did they look like?" asked the Fisherman.

"Foreign," said Agatha. "Want to stay over?"

"Sorry, got an early morning," he said, as he left.

Agatha looked sad as he left. But Agatha always looked sad.

Chapter 40

The Russians pay a visit

A few days after he returned from the Rip, there was a knock at the door. Several surly, swarthy men in black suits stood silently on the doorstep. He could see tattoos peaking above their collars and below the cuffs. They were men who meant business and were not afraid to do it. In a thick accent the main bloke asked him if he knew a man called Vladimir.

"Never heard of him," said the Fisherman.

All the men in black suits had bulges under the left arm, he had seen enough crime movies and enough war to know that they had guns in holsters and were happy to use them. He was less confrontational than he might have been, although if the truth be known, he was sweating like a pig. But he did not want them to know that. The lead thug stared at him with inscrutable, black, Russian eyes. The Fisherman stared back with his best thousand yard stare. After a time, they left with suspicious glares and menacing looks.

The Fisherman closed the door and leaned back against it exhaling deeply. He felt that he had dodged a bullet, literally. There was a soft knock on the door, he reached for the bait knife. Dropping his hand behind his back he opened the door. It had been concealed in the waist band of his pants under his shirt. He had planned to kill the man who knocked on the door until he had seen that there were several of them and they had murderous inclinations. He dropped his hand, behind his back, concealing the bait knife, razor sharp. He steeled himself and opened the door, intent on killing whosoever had knocked on the door.

The Russians had returned, he thought, and there was no going back. He had been in tough spots before, Vietnam and other places the government would never admit. He did not want trouble on his doorstep, but he knew these men had come to kill him and he would not shy away from it. He opened the door quickly knife in his hand poised behind the door. Oleg stood in the dim light, a small pistol fitted with a silencer in his hand.

"Where the fuck did you come from?" asked the Fisherman.

"Out of the bushes," said Oleg.

"No shit Sherlock," said the Fisherman.

"What is Sherlock?" asked Oleg.

"Come inside," said the Fisherman impatiently. "I thought you had gone to Eucumbene," said the Fisherman.

"I thought I would stay a few days, I knew they would come here," said Oleg.

"Nice of you to tell me," said the Fisherman somewhat testily. "I could have used your help a few minutes ago," the Fisherman added.

"It was fine, things were okay, and I do not like to do another boat trip, so I do not kill them," said Oleg.

"Fuck you, they could have killed me," said the Fisherman.

"If they had wanted you dead then you would be dead. It is better this way, they think you know nothing," said Oleg.

"Fuck you," said the Fisherman. Oleg looked hurt and busied himself tucking the gun under his shirt.

"They will not return," he said. "I go to Eucumbene now," he said.

He walked out of the hall and into the darkness disappearing in a ghost like way.

"See you when I see you," said the Fisherman into the darkness.

There was no reply. Oleg was gone, at least for present purposes. The Fisherman closed the door and made a cup of tea although he felt uneasy. He did not sleep well that night, waiting for a knock on the door which never came.

THE END

Acknowledgments

Bernard Holbery, photographer, fly fisher and charcutier extraordinaire is the author of the cover photograph.
Thank you.

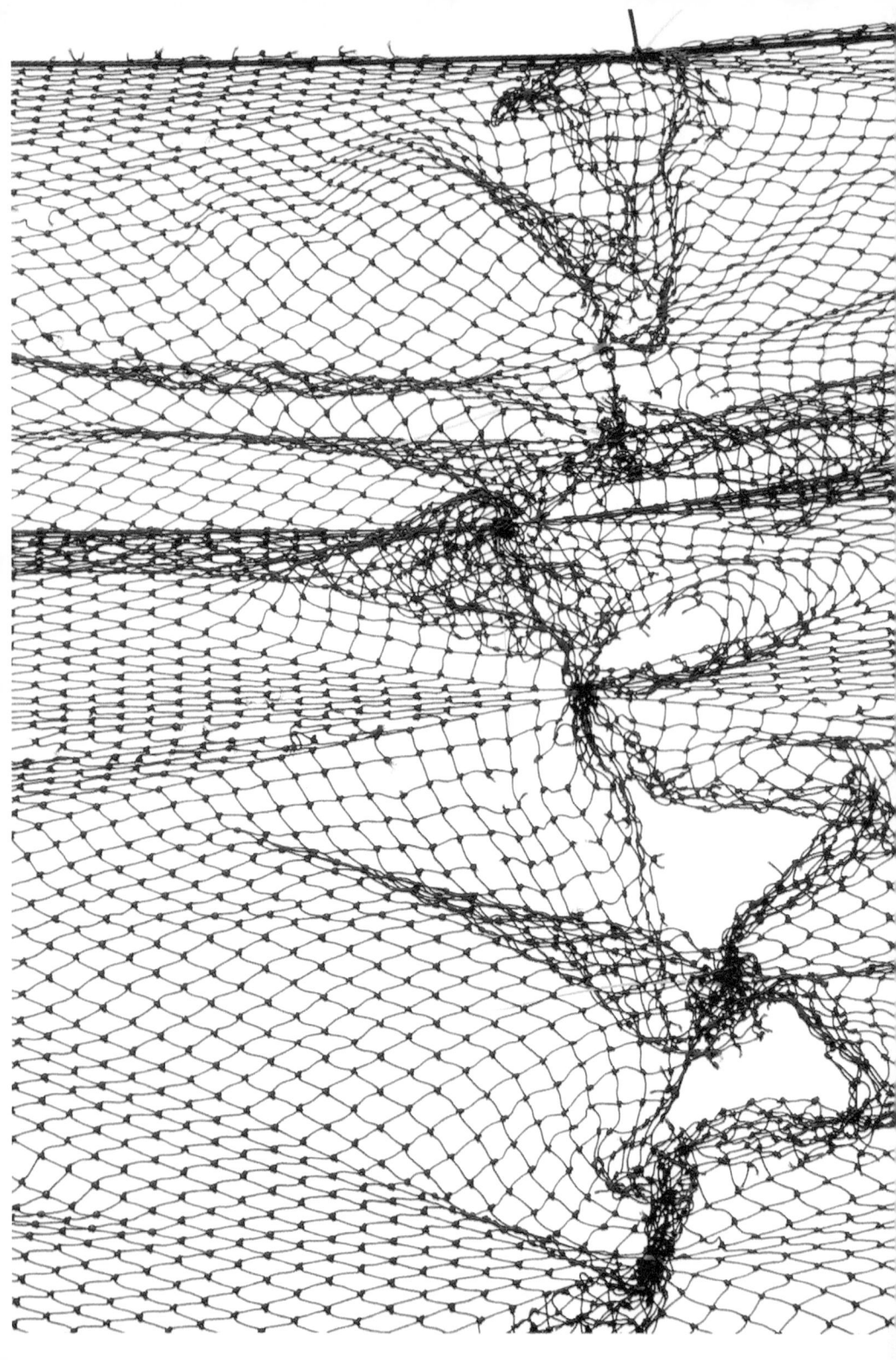

www.ingramcontent.com/pod-product-compliance
Lightning Source LLC
Chambersburg PA
CBHW021104080526
44587CB00010B/378